The Vital Questions Series

CLEAR THINKING FOR FAITHFUL LIVING

□ □

These books investigate key issues that make a practical difference in how Christians think and act. The goal is to provide a substantial, acccssible discussion of issues about which Christians need to know more. This series is intended as a service to the church and to individuals with the aim of better preparing a "Christian mind," resulting in more faithful living.

Daniel Taylor, General Editor

How
Shall We
Worship?

Biblical Guidelines for the Worship Wars

□ □ □ □ □ □ □ □ □ □ □ □ □ □   MARVA J. DAWN

DANIEL TAYLOR, GENERAL EDITOR

Tyndale House Publishers, Inc., Wheaton, Illinois

Visit Tyndale's exciting Web site at www.tyndale.com

How Shall *We Worship? Biblical Guidelines for the Worship Wars*

Copyright © 2003 by Marva J. Dawn. All rights reserved.

Edited by Daniel Taylor and MaryLynn Layman

Designed by Kelly Bennema with Luke Daab

Library of Congress Cataloging-in-Publication Data

Dawn, Marva J.
 How shall we worship? : biblical guidelines for the worship wars / Marva J. Dawn ; Daniel Taylor, general editor.
  p. cm.
Includes bibliographical references and index.
 ISBN 0-8423-5636-3 (hc)
 1. Public worship. I. Taylor, Daniel, 1948- II. Title.
BV15.D375 2003
264—dc21   2002155584

Printed in the United States of America

07 06 05 04 03
 7   6   5   4   3 2   1

This book is dedicated to

*All those who know that Christians are in exile,
yet hear the Kingdom's music
and dance to it now,
And especially to Lefty and Tom,
who taught me to worship
and who continue to worship
in spite of debilitating affliction.*

Contents

Introduction

Most of my happiest memories from early childhood relate to worship. Since my father was the
church organist and the director of choirs, our
family was always present for worship whenever
the congregation offered it.

There was always great anticipation in our
household for worship. Saturday nights meant I
actually had my hair pinned up after my bath,
and we always set out my Sunday-best clothes for
the next morning. If it was Christmas or Easter,
we had been hearing Dad composing new pieces
throughout the preparatory seasons of Advent
and Lent, and every week my father delighted in
practicing the organ and directing choir rehears-
als. I'll never forget the thrill when I first played
the final pedal note on the organ at the end of
worship (I had *practiced* with Dad!) and, several
years later, my delight the first time he invited
me to write a text for his new music.

Worship was always filled with glorious sights
and sounds. Our church building had an intri-

cately carved altar, ancient Christian symbols everywhere, and beautiful stained-glass windows that reminded me of whole stories in the Bible. We sang all kinds of music—new and old—often with various students playing their brass instruments or flutes. What I saw and what I heard in worship throughout my childhood deeply formed my faith and my enraptured desire to praise God with all my heart and mind, voice and life.

I *loved* worship! Especially I loved the singing and often memorized hymns as part of my memory work assignments in the Lutheran school (where Mom was secretary, Dad was principal, and they were my fourth- and eighth-grade teachers). I'd sing those songs at the top of my lungs while I did my newspaper route. (My customers always knew when their paper had arrived.)

I still love worship. For many years I have sung in choirs and folk teams and directed them, have played various instruments and (more recently) have preached for worship. When I was a junior in college, I participated in a choir that sang Christian concerts literally around the world; in the last few years I have taught in numerous nations and thereby have experienced a multitude of worldwide riches in worship.

With such a background of precious—and global—worship, I find it piercingly painful that in so many places people fight about it. The dissensions take many forms, but often erupt in bitter battles over styles of music or aspects of divergent tastes. In response, I try to help people ask deeper questions, get to the root of the issues, look to the Scriptures for as much insight into God's desires as we can gather.

Let's ask some of those questions together, shall we? For example, what is worship? Let's begin by realizing that it is our glad response to the immense grace of the Triune God. All of life is worship if we live in gratitude and reverence, with mindfulness of God and eagerness to serve Him.

At particular times, we expressly worship with words, songs, and actions of thanks and petition and praise. When we do this by ourselves, we engage in the practices of private worship or devotions. If we gather with other Christians, we participate in public, corporate worship. The result will be that we become more

Let's begin by realizing that worship is our glad response to the immense grace of the Triune God.

deeply formed to worship God in all we think, say, or do in daily life.

This poem by Abraham Joshua Heschel suggests many questions we could ponder:

Amidst the meditation of mountains, the humility
of flowers—
wiser than all alphabets—
clouds that die constantly for the sake of His glory,
we are hating, hunting, hurting . . .
Only one response can maintain us: gratefulness
for witnessing the wonder,
for the gift of our unearned right to serve,
to adore, and to fulfill.[1]

Is the public, corporate worship of our churches true to the Christian faith? Does it form its participants with the humility and wisdom of God's creation? What can we learn from nature about praising God? Does our worship enable us to be ready to die for the sake of God's glory? Does it cleanse us from our propensity to hate, hunt, hurt? Does it help us witness God's glory and nourish in us gratefulness? wonder? Does it stir us to witness, service, adoration, fulfillment of God's purposes?

The Crux of the Problem

Worship is a much-debated subject in twenty-first-century North America. In the past three or four decades, many churches have had bitter fights over worship issues, and many congregations have split internally or externally. In the present, thank God, it seems that more church leaders and congregations are trying to ask deeper questions and to think through the issues more biblically and theologically and ecclesiologically.

What kinds of questions could and should we be asking for the sake of genuine worship? Could any of the questions in the following paragraphs bring some clarity to the issues in your congregation?

First of all, we have to recognize that many members of our churches do not know what worship is. How shall we sing the LORD's song in this strange land? How should churches conduct their worship in the midst of a culture that less and less knows what worship is? How might congregations nurture in their members deeper insight into the meaning and practice of worship?

What does it mean to worship? What would be

the answer if we asked Christians who worship with you why they are there? Would their answers be biblically formed—or would they primarily reveal the influences of the culture that surrounds the Church?[2]

Simultaneously we must also ask, why do congregations seem so often to be fighting over worship and music, styles and forms? To end the battles, some churches start multiple services, with two or more styles featured at separate times and labeled with such terms as "contemporary" or "traditional" or "blended/convergent." Other churches specialize in a certain kind of "praise and worship" or advertise their services as "exciting" and "upbeat." Do these descriptions and understandings enable churches to be all that they could be for the sake of the world around them?

Why don't our churches seem to be affecting our culture? Why do so many who say they are "spiritual" want nothing to do with our churches' worship?

Why don't our typical Sunday morning worship services cause us to tremble? Are we really encountering God?

We could ask many other questions—and will be doing so as this book progresses. I begin with these because in teaching throughout North America and across denominational lines I have discovered that many of the arguments and fights about worship could be avoided if we asked **W**hy don't our churches seem to be affecting our culture? better questions—and if we let our biblical roots and the branches of the Church on Christ the Vine bear fruit.

It seemed that the best way to organize our discussion of the issues would be to take a biblical text and thoroughly consider its implications for our worship decisions. Psalm 96, an "enthronement" psalm used in the worship of Israel, provides an excellent structure for asking key questions. (The entire psalm appears on the following page for your reference.)

Psalm 96

A Call to Worship the Lord the Righteous Judge.

Sing to the Lord a new song;
  Sing to the Lord, all the earth.

2 Sing to the Lord, bless His name;
  Proclaim good tidings of His salvation from day to day.

3 Tell of His glory among the nations,
  His wonderful deeds among all the peoples.

4 For great is the Lord, and greatly to be praised;
  He is to be feared above all gods.

5 For all the gods of the peoples are idols,
  But the Lord made the heavens.

6 Splendor and majesty are before Him,
  Strength and beauty are in His sanctuary.

7 Ascribe to the Lord, O families of the peoples,
  Ascribe to the Lord glory and strength.

8 Ascribe to the Lord the glory of His name;
  Bring an offering, and come into His courts.

9 Worship the Lord in holy attire;
  Tremble before Him, all the earth.

10 Say among the nations, "The Lord reigns;
  Indeed, the world is firmly established, it will not be moved;
  He will judge the peoples with equity."

11 Let the heavens be glad, and let the earth rejoice;
  Let the sea roar, and all it contains;

12 Let the field exult, and all that is in it.
  Then all the trees of the forest will sing for joy

13 Before the Lord, for He is coming;
  For He is coming to judge the earth.

He will judge the world in righteousness,
  And the peoples in His faithfulness.

1 What Kinds of Music Should We Use?

Sing to the LORD a new song;

PSALM 96:1a

Since my father was an organist, choir director, and composer, I grew up loving both new music which he created and old music which he treasured and sometimes rearranged. As a child, I observed his great love for worship and for music of all sorts—which inevitably rubbed off and kindled in me the same desire to praise God with the best texts and tunes we can invent or pass on from our forebears in the faith. Consequently, it still seems strange to me that churches fight over styles and hastily reject the Church's heritage without investigating its riches or refuse to use global music and new songs without exploring their possibilities.

Some churches are founded upon the principle that only "contemporary" music—particularly that which matches the styles of the culture around us—should be used for worship. Verses such as Psalm 96:1a seem to justify that decision. However, this first verse doesn't suggest using *only* new songs, for later in the same psalm its poet employs an older song from Israel's heritage. Verses 7-8a of Psalm 96 quote the more ancient beginning of Psalm 29 (and 1 Chronicles 16 repeats Psalm 96 or perhaps antedates it). Those who advocate only "contemporary" worship miss the fact that worship throughout the Scriptures makes use of both new and old materials. To sing new songs doesn't negate singing old songs, too. In fact, we must consider what is lost if our worship has no connection to the "cloud of witnesses" who have preceded us in faith.

In many church situations I have found worshipers fighting for "contemporary" worship without really knowing what they mean by that vocabulary. The term *contemporary* is usually not defined. Do we mean by that word something that sounds like a pop radio station, or a brand-new organ improvisation, or a new text set to an old melody, or a new melody put to an old text, or an ancient song newly arranged and freshly contemplated? All those possibilities are "contemporary." Are we arguing for a certain instrumentation or a certain adaptation to culture? Ironically, some of the churches that boast of always singing "new songs" sing them over and over week after week and repetitively in each service, so that their newness is hastily worn off.

On the other side of many worship conflicts, some people advocate using only "traditional" music. That term isn't very helpful either because it doesn't clarify to which traditions we are referring. Do we mean Swedish or Swahili traditions, hymns or chants, the ancient liturgy of the Church or revised liturgies from the Calvinist or Lutheran or Anglican reformers? Do we mean the traditions from the first centuries of the pre-Constantinian Church or those from more recent American reformation movements?

It is essential that we ask what people mean by the words *traditional* and *contemporary* because failure to define them clearly usually leads to unnecessary arguments. Moreover, often the terms are used in response to wrong questions or as wrong answers to good questions, as we will see

> It is essential that we ask what people mean by the words *traditional* and *contemporary* because failure to define them clearly usually leads to unnecessary arguments.

3

more thoroughly below. At this point it is important simply to recognize the importance of both new and old.

Throughout the history of the people of God, worship has made use of a mixture of elements old and new. Many songs in the Old Testament (or First Testament) make use of older elements from Israel's history. Songs in the book of Revelation use phrases from the Psalms and Isaiah. Both Ephesians 5:19 and Colossians 3:16 urge us to teach and admonish with "psalms and hymns and spiritual songs." These texts free us from debating about musical styles and suggest instead a wide range of music for our faithfulness.

The word *psalms* invites us to participate with our Jewish and Christian forebears in singing the Old Testament poems, written for synagogue and Temple (as indicated by the frequent title, "To the Chief Musician" or "For the choir director") and collected primarily in the book of Psalms (and also in other poetic portions, most notably Isaiah).

The biblical term *hymns* points to the development of specifically Christian songs in the traditions of faith. The New Testament contains many of the earliest hymns, such as Philippians 2:5-11, 1 Timothy 3:16, 2 Timothy 2:11-13, John 1:1-14, and all the hymns in the book of Revelation, such as 5:9-10, 12, and 13. Similarly, today there are many hymns held in common by diverse denominations and eras—and written by great saints from Ambrose of Milan (339–397) and Bernard of Clairvaux (1090–1153) to Martin Luther (1483–1546) and John Wesley (1703–1791).

The phrase *spiritual songs* cannot be specifically defined. Perhaps it refers to new expressions of praise composed at the moment, or ecstatic utterances, or perhaps local music. Though we don't know exactly what the phrase originally signified, we can be reminded by it now that God is never contained by the music we already know. There will always be a need for new melodies, new harmonies, new texts, new arrangements, new instrumentations, new expressions of, and to, the infinitely incomprehensible God—even as we will always build on the faith expressions of our forebears and need some of the old, old songs to tell "the old, old story."

As we look at various stages in the history of Christianity, we discover that the sixteenth-century Reformers usually valued the past, even as they discovered the new. The earliest Christians patterned their worship after Jewish synagogue services, but added to them the celebration of the Lord's Supper. Martin Luther kept the Mass from the Catholic church, but put it into the people's native tongue. John Wesley continued to worship in the Anglican church, even as he and his brother Charles wrote many new hymns.

The Antithesis: Separation

Because the Church has generally used its treasures old and new, it was odd that in the last decades of the twentieth century churches started advertising a specific kind of music (usually "contemporary" or "traditional") for their worship services or that they split their worshiping Body into two or more different styles of services offered at different times. This leads to all sorts of divisions—by age, musical taste, head and heart, doctrine and feelings.

Are such divisions good for churches? We have seen, from Ephesians and Colossians, that such sundering might not be biblically appropriate. But do the advantages of such partitioning outweigh the disadvantages? Does it solve some problems? Is it really spiritually helpful? Before answering those questions, we must understand a little more history—both long range and from the past half century.

If we look over twenty centuries of church history, we glimpse many periods when movements of renewal broke away from the mainstream churches. Monastic currents shed some of the unbiblical accretions (especially wealth) that had invaded Christianity. Pietistic streams stressing Bible study and personal religious experience protested secular power structures or excessively intellectualized instruction in state churches.

The latter highlights a particular pair that has caused conflicts noticeable in many eras: the opposition of objective and subjective, expressions of truth about God and feelings in response to God. The dominant fight between "traditional" and "contemporary" sometimes circles around this opposition, for the older traditional hymns (with such exceptions as nineteenth-century romantic pieces) are typically more doctrinally focused, whereas a greater proportion of contemporary music stresses feelings primarily. It seems to be an opposition of truth and spirit, though Jesus underscored that "true worshipers shall worship the Father in spirit *and* truth" (John 4:23, emphasis mine).

Can our churches ask better questions so that the music we use in worship enables us to be both filled and free with the Spirit and also grounded in biblical and doctrinal truth? Without the emotion and willingness of Spirit, our music becomes dry and dusty—without life. Without doctrinal bones as a skeleton, the Body is not enfleshed in a healthy way.

It is essential that our worship music—as well as all the other formative elements of our congregation's life—continuously holds in tension the opposite necessities of both Spirit and truth. These two form a dialectical pair, for they are both important but seem to be pulling in different directions. How can we keep them both prominent and balanced? Since the truth side of this dialectic is less likely to be accentuated these days, let me elaborate that dimension.

> **It is essential that our worship music continuously holds in tension the opposite necessities of both Spirit and truth.**

I have a crooked leg that offers an excellent visual aid for the importance of straight doctrinal bones as the foundation for worship. I wear a toe-to-knee plastic brace to hold my leg firm because otherwise, if I put full weight on the leg, the bone would probably snap at the place where it is bent. Similarly, churches who have crooked doctrine—for example, an inadequate trinitarianism—will snap when that which is awry comes under pressure. Moreover, holding my crooked leg stable by means of plastic isn't a good solution either, for often the meeting of bones and plastic on two sides of fragile skin rubs ulcerated wounds. (I have just begun walking again after 15 months on crutches.) Similarly, churches who try to prop up their crooked doctrinal structure with supports from the outside might chafe incurable wounds.

Many formerly powerful churches have fallen apart or have become seriously weakened either from snapping at the crooked places or from festering wounds that can't be healed. For example, churches that use essentially narcissistic music, focused on self rather than God, find it increasingly difficult to engage members in service and outreach. Churches whose music accentuates only the Holy Spirit, thus betraying deficient trinitarianism, often have an insufficient doctrine of confession and forgiveness and consequently find it difficult to deal with conflicts. The freedom of the Spirit must be matched with the discipline of the Truth—especially in contrast with, and resistance to, the world's untruths.

Recent Escalations of Separation

In all of history, both unifying and dividing forces have been at work, with one or the other prevailing. In the last half century, however, the powers of separation have been more intensely aggravated by a combination of factors. We have to understand the history of church music as it is intertwined with the rebellions of the '60s and the development of "niche marketing."

I do not intend to romanticize the past (every era has its flaws), but in general before the second half of the twentieth century in North America music unified diverse peoples. Families would cluster around the piano and sing all kinds of songs—hymns, folk songs, patriotic marches, show tunes, lullabies. Literature and art often portray families gathering in the parlor or communities assembling in the town hall and playing a great variety of music on a wide assortment of instruments, often homemade.

One strong element that contributed to present fractures was the cluster of changes, events, and attitudes of the '60s. The large postwar population bubble coming of age, the development of junior high schools in which teens were mentored by their peers rather than by a consistent teacher, escalating anger about the Vietnam War, violent governmental crackdowns like the Kent State killings of student protesters, an unprecedented rejection of elders' authority by teenagers, and new infusions of illegal drugs were some factors that intensified the separation of young and old. Music in the '60s became an identity marker, a sign of rebellion, a unifier of one segment in protest against all the rest of the culture, a means for flaunting independence.

At the same time, businesses—particularly the record industry—realized that they could make much more money if they divided people up into smaller and smaller niches. Instead of one radio station playing all kinds of music, we could have numerous stations, each with a specialty. Various newspapers in Canada and the U.S. have featured articles on the new "tween market" (ages 9–13), for which a special line of cosmetics, a new fashion magazine, new movies and games have been designed. "Tweens" have their own styles and models, trends and tunes because the producers and marketers have discovered that they have $1.4 billion to spend.

Bring the same sort of rebellion (against the institution of the Church and its practices) and of niche marketing ("We want *our* kind of music") into our congregations, and is it any wonder that the splitting of churches into various styles of worship should intensify dramatically with the boomer generation?

Both sides erred when the boomer generation rebelled against the music of the churches and demanded their own styles, like "Praise and Worship." The traditionalists blundered in not finding ways to incorporate new sounds and to ask better questions for sorting the new music. The contemporaryists misjudged in not learning from their elders better practices of teaching and leading new music, of filling songs with better theology, of matching sound to meaning.

By God's grace, more and more churches—across the denominational spectrum and around the globe—seem to be asking better questions. Some are inquiring how we can avoid these splits, how various styles can be brought together. Many of the younger-than-boomer generations are asking what might be learned from the past, from the roots of the Church, as they search for mystery, symbolism, heritage, and depth—all for the sake of worshiping God genuinely in "spirit and truth."

Not "Blended" or "Convergent," but a Sense of the Whole Church

My primary reason for wanting churches to use many musical styles and sounds in their worship is because we have such a big God. No single type of music can respond to all that God is. No instrument can sing all God's attributes. No era of the Church has displayed the fullness of God's glory.

Some persons seek these days to offer what is called "blended" worship, in which old and new music are featured. This is an excellent goal, though I have trouble with the name *blended,* since recovering from emergency jaw surgery once necessitated that for three months I eat food made soft in the blender. That illustration points out the danger: If we use music from different eras and styles, we dare not let the songs played in "blended" worship services all sound the same and become indistinguishably gray like various foods tossed together in the blender. Instead, we will want to be very careful that each

13

piece maintains its own character and is sung with its own integrity.

The adjective *convergent* has often been used, too, especially in association with Robert Webber's idea of "Ancient-Future" faith.[3] This, too, represents an excellent goal, for it emphasizes that we have to get back to the Church's roots if we want truly to understand what worship is and how our praises might be sung. One helpful question the term raises is at what point the convergence takes place. Do we mean that all the worship of the past converges in our present moment of worship?

Perhaps we could be clearer about the nature of our faith if we remember that worship converges ultimately in that great day when God brings to culmination the Triune work of reconciling the cosmos. At that glorious time, all of our present-day worship will converge with all the praise of all the saints throughout time and space when we join the heavenly host in their eternal and perfect worship. (We will return to this emphasis at the end of this book.)

Meanwhile, how can we make use of more of the best music—old and new? It is critical that we decide what we employ not by the criteria of what we like or what will please certain people or what will attract the neighbors or what matches the most people's tastes.[4] Future questions in this book will give better criteria for making our decisions. Perhaps we can simply summarize our goal by declaring that our worship could make use of "the Music of the 'one holy, catholic, apostolic Church' (as the Nicene Creed calls it) for the Sake of the Whole World." Our desire is that all our music will help believers learn the language of faith and the nature of true worship.

For example, one Sunday at an African-American congregation to which I belonged, the service incorporated a great diversity of styles of music, not because we worried about using such an assortment, but because all the pieces we sang captured well the Scripture texts for the day and the season of the church year in which we were worshiping. At the beginning we sang two

Our desire is that all our music will help believers learn the language of faith and the nature of true worship.

black spirituals and one so-called "contemporary chorus." The Old Testament lesson that day was Isaiah 12, so for the children's sermon the whole congregation learned the Hebrew-melody song,

"Behold, God Is My Salvation," while I taught the children a Jewish dance. The Epistle lesson that day stressed the immensity of God's grace, so we sang the early American hymn, "There's a Wideness in God's Mercy." We tuned all the strings of a guitar to Es and Bs, and one person strummed it to produce a droning while we sang the verses with Appalachian-style "call and response."

The Gospel text was Luke 15, the story of the Prodigal Son (or the Waiting Father), which is wonderfully captured and applied to us in Kevin Nichols' text, "Our Father, We Have Wandered," copyrighted by the International Committee on English in the Liturgy and available in many denominational hymnals. The second verse of this stunning text ends, "In haste you come to meet us and home rejoicing bring, in gladness there to greet us with calf and robe and ring." What a humbling text to remind us of how unworthy we are to worship God! The three stanzas of Nichols' poem are set to the melody, "Herzlich tut mich verlangen," most often associated with the chorale, "O Sacred Head Now Wounded," and harmonized by Johann Sebastian Bach (one of five orchestrations of that tune in his *St. Matthew Passion*).

Each piece we sang in worship that day fit in with the whole service, because they were all chosen to display the texts of the day and the theme of the entire service. Though many different styles were represented, each piece was accompanied according to its unique style, so that all the music was experienced with its own integrity. All together, the songs offered a great example of having the whole Church present in our worship. The music included Jewish and Gentile, black and white, ancient texts and new texts, old and new melodies. It knit the people of our community together—black and white, young and old, richer and poorer, new Christians and those more mature in faith.

II Who Is Being Worshiped?

Sing to the LORD, all the earth.

PSALM 96:1b

The greatest danger of choosing where or at which type of service we worship according to our musical taste is that we forget that worship is for God. The poet of Psalm 96 calls "all the earth" to sing to the LORD because God deserves the praise of all His creation.

Notice that in this psalm the name LORD is entirely capitalized. This is the customary practice in English Bibles when the Hebrew word to be translated is the name *YHWH*, which is often vocalized (when it *is* vocalized; Orthodox Jews still do not say this name) as *Yahweh* (formerly as *Jehovah*) and which is drawn from the verb root meaning "to be." That is the name by which the LORD revealed Himself to Moses at the burning bush in Exodus 3:14-15. It is a term that distinguishes Him from all the neighboring, false deities. He is not just any god, but He alone is the faithful covenant God, the great "I AM."

That name gives us a special reason to sing, for it calls us to amazement at all the precious promises given by this LORD, to trust because this LORD is constantly faithful to His covenant, and to thankfulness for His effective deliverance of His people from all their captivities. When we worship, we sing to the LORD because of who God is—and God is so astounding that He deserves our worship whether we feel like offering it or not.

> **W**hen we worship, we sing to the LORD because of who God is—and God is so astounding that He deserves our worship whether we feel like offering it or not.

This raises a critical question: How has it come about that so many Christians have forgotten that worship is for God? We will look at two pivotal reasons, one from individual believers and one from congregations. Both are ultimately due to sin.

Social analyst Christopher Lasch called this "The Culture of Narcissism" and emphasized that the end of the twentieth century produced a momentous selfishness (still evident today) less prompted by larger concerns and by care for others than ever before.[5] In addition, this is the age of marketing, characterized by an endless barrage of advertisements inviting us to pamper ourselves with countless new fads and fashions. Our technological society relentlessly immerses us in continuously proliferating commodities. Aren't you appalled by the boundless plethora of products and services available—as if just one more thing could finally satisfy our ceaselessly voracious desires?

Even if we resist the materialistic consumerism of our era, we cannot avoid its incessant pressures. We can't turn our heads without seeing more ads; the media are everywhere in waiting rooms and airports, on airwaves and lightwaves; the malls are mushrooming over the landscape; telephone salespeople disrupt our work and home life.

Unless we are perpetually vigilant, we find ourselves asking about everything, "What's in it for me?" When that point of view invades our worship attitudes, we complain, "I didn't get much out of that worship service."

So what? It wasn't you we were worshiping, was it?

How we *feel* about worship actually is not the point. Worship is for God, because creatures owe their Creator praise. All the earth responds to God's gift of being, as Abraham Joshua Heschel's lines at the beginning of this book suggested, but human beings—stuck in our sinfulness—respond with "hunting" for what will please ourselves.

A second major reason (a corporate one) for our forgetting that worship is for God is that declining church attendance and decreasing denominational membership have caused many churches to ask the wrong questions. Instead of examining how best the worshiping community can praise and glorify God, they began to inquire, "What can we do in worship to attract the unbeliever?" Consequently, numerous congregations made radical worship changes that arose from and reflected panic more than wisdom.

Marketing gurus took advantage of this panic and published numerous books about how certain worship forms could attract unbelievers. Willow Creek Church, which offers laudatory evangelistic events on Sunday mornings and worship for believers on Wednesday nights, has often been falsely imitated by churches who turn their Sunday morning worship services into evangelistic rallies—and forget that worship is owed to God and not the neighbor.

Meanwhile, other congregations, noticing that they were forfeiting members to the "more attractive" churches, suddenly changed how they worshiped in order not to lose their share of the market. Though more and more research is demonstrating that "church growth" has been somewhat of a mirage because over 90 percent of it has simply been Christians moving from one congregation to another, many congregations still think that worship issues should be decided on the basis of the "appeal" factor. How, then, will individuals and communities learn again that worship is for God?

III ▌ How *Do* We Worship God?

Sing to the LORD, bless His name;

PSALM 96:2a

The third line of Psalm 96 gives us some direction
for how we worship God when it adds the parallel
phrase, "bless His name." How do we bless the
LORD, and what is the significance of His name? It
will be more understandable if we look at the latter first.

In biblical texts the word *name* connotes more
than simply one's moniker. The term suggests the
character that the name represents. That is why
God changed Jacob's name to Israel, as he developed from primarily a "supplanter" for his own
benefit to "one who strives with God" (Genesis
25:26 and 32:28).

God's various names hint at different dimensions of the Triune attributes and interventions.
The names are more than merely images and met-
aphors, for God really is Light, Truth, Love, and

so forth, but we dare not confine ourselves to what we know humanly about those terms. One important case is the name *Father,* which we call the First Person of the Trinity because the incarnate Jesus, who was truly man, born of the Virgin Mary, as our High Priest introduces us into His own intimacy with His Father. However, we dare not reduce that name to our human ideas of the gender of one parent, since God is beyond gender. To bless God's name, *Father,* is to bow before the mystery and wonder of the incarnation, of the possibility that we can participate in the Triune intimacy, and of the fullness of the protection and provision our heavenly Father offers to His children. To pray our Lord Jesus' prayer is to bless God's name.

Doesn't it seem strange that so often biblical passages invite or command us to "bless" God or God's name, since God is the one always blessing us? Without doubt He doesn't need our blessing. Do our praises do anything for Him? Perhaps we bless God with an ulterior motive—that God would bless us back! Does our worship have such utilitarian goals?

In fact, if we are really blessing God, truly praising Him, we have to recognize that our worship is fundamentally useless (in the world's terms). The verb calling us to bless God's name is an imperative urging us to kneel, to adore the LORD with bended knee. The entire phrase proclaims that we should salute God's character or pay homage because God deserves our gratitude.

> **T**he verb calling us to bless God's name is an imperative urging us to kneel, to adore the LORD with bended knee.

Notice that the focus is entirely on God and says nothing about us or usefulness. As soon as we can stop making worship utilitarian (primarily in the current push to make worship "attractive" in order to "appeal" to new members), then we might get back to genuine worshiping.

It is actually unproductive to bless God—God doesn't need it, and it won't change God's opinion about us one whit. Moreover, if we are selfless enough truly to sing to or of *YHWH*, it might not even make us feel any better. But we will be changed by it if we respond earnestly and wholeheartedly to all that God is.

Perhaps it will help us to imagine how we bless God's name by considering the opposite, to befoul or revile it. When I was a child, I didn't want to do anything that would besmirch my father's name because he was the school principal—and a very good one. Similarly, we who believe that God is a gracious and merciful Father want to live as graced, mercied people, lest we defame Him.

Do we live up to the name *Christian,* "little Christ"? Does the character we exhibit in our daily lives bless His name or blacken it? Do we honor God's name or malign it by the way we worship? If we engage in our supposed "worship" only to make ourselves feel good, are we exalting the Holy Spirit's name or denigrating it?

I have used examples both from the public, corporate worship of God's people and also from daily life, because one goal of our worship services is to equip church members for recognizing all of their lives as worship. The first three lines of Psalm 96 can refer to singing in worship services and/or singing to the LORD with our daily lives, for "the earth" is always praising God with its being. The Hebrew word *ha-aretz* is used throughout the Old Testament to signify "the land," and numerous poetic images (including some at the end of Psalm 96) show us the holy land singing by producing its crops and providing a home for God's people. Do we sing to God with all our being? Do our practices of public, corporate wor-

ship and private, personal devotions form us to
be people who *live* praise?

The Church Year as a Vehicle to Bless God's Name More Fully

Because God's character is infinitely beyond our
comprehension and expression and because God
has intervened into our lives and world so thoroughly, we can never bless the Trinity's name adequately. One tool developed by the Church to
widen our song is the church year.

Many churches in North America have rejected the use of the church year as part of a general rejection of things "Catholic." Those who
emphasize that worship must be "contemporary"
and "appealing to the public" often think that the
church year is detrimental to those goals. The season of Lent, for example, is criticized as being too
morose and not in tune with the attempt to make
worship "upbeat."

The problem with such rejection, however, is
that it diminishes our understanding of God, for
the sufferings and passion of Jesus are essential
elements of God's character and interventions on
our behalf and should be commemorated appropriately. Worship can't always be upbeat if we

are worshiping the LORD in all God's Triune fullness. Furthermore, sufferings and trials also characterize human life, and believers need to learn
the language of faith
for finding God in the
midst of our trials and
for being able to ex-
press our sorrows and
hopes. Most important, we need Lent to face up
to the depth of our sinfulness and how incapable
we are of saving ourselves. How ever will we
understand the lengths to which Jesus went for
our sakes if we don't spend time grasping the true
nature of our fallenness and the fullness of
Christ's atoning work?

Worship can't always be
upbeat if we are worshiping
the LORD in all God's
Triune fullness.

The earliest Christians realized that the Passion
and Resurrection of Christ changed *everything,*
that all time now drew its meaning from His
salvific work on our behalf. Consequently, they
remembered and more deeply commemorated the
Passion of Christ, His rising from the dead, and
the pouring out of the Spirit each year as the
Jewish Passover came around. There is evidence
that as early as the second century A.D. the Jewish
calendar of Pascha and Pentecost feasts was already beginning to be gradually transformed into

the Christian calendar of Passion, Easter, and Pentecost festivals. Then this calendar began to be expanded when, for example, the Council of Nicaea in 325 established the forty-day season of Lent.

It is not necessary here to recount the historical development of the entire church year, nor to detail its elements thoroughly since many resources provide that information.[6] What is important for us to recognize is that more and more churches are rediscovering the great gifts provided by this tool—one of the most important of which is that it enables us to bless God's name more thoroughly.

The season of Advent, which begins the church year, starts four Sundays before Christmas and extends to Christmas. Its main themes are repentance, waiting, preparation, and Joy.[7] It is an essential gift in a society plagued with arrogance, instant gratification, lack of forethought, and insatiable desires.

Worship in this season forces us to ask whether we are ready for the Christ Child. Do we know how much we need a Savior? Do we see how much our society with its injustice for the poor and its militarization violates God's design for wholeness and peace in the world? Just this week I read a politically conservative news magazine that admitted that many nations of the world resent the U.S. and consider it the "Roman empire of the new millennium." When Mary sings her Magnificat in Luke 1—the Gospel text assigned for the last Sunday of Advent in the lectionary (or schedule of Scripture readings) which many denominations have adopted in common—do we realize that her phrase, "[He] has sent the rich away empty" (Luke 1:53, NIV), describes us in relation to the rest of the world? Other texts for Advent, especially those from Isaiah, remind us that the Messiah governs with righteousness—and thereby add to our formation as people seeking to build justice in the world.

The third Sunday of Advent interrupts the season's predominant mood of repentance with a celebration of Joy. (Many denominations signify this by using purple candles to signify repentance on the first, second, and fourth Sundays of Advent, but a pink candle, representing Joy, on the third Sunday.) After two weeks of recognizing that we are sinful human beings who desperately need a Savior, this day of rejoicing reminds us that God has been merciful to us in sending us the Son. That heightens our anticipation for the day when Christ will come again, when once again Triune mercy will be showered upon us as we are received into the eternal kingdom.

I have briefly sketched these dispositions of Advent because they reveal how valuable the church year is for highlighting dimensions of faith we might not always think about. Our worship is made much richer with understandings of various dimensions of God's complexity and with far deeper insights into our human condition when we let the nature of each particular season guide our choices of songs, accompaniments, texts, sermon themes, prayers, dramas, art.

Christmas is a season known by the world, but poorly practiced. It is usually conceived in sentimentally nostalgic forms, and rarely do we recognize the immense humility and condescension of Jesus that He came to this earth. Does our worship remind us of His poverty, His suffering, His profound humanity, the danger that began with King Herod and accompanied Him all His life?

Our worship is made much richer when we let the nature of each particular season guide our choices of songs, accompaniments, texts, sermon themes, prayers, dramas, art.

Space prevents us from looking even sketchily at the rest of the church year, but think of the outstanding possibilities for blessing the LORD's name which could be found if our churches would all practice the seasons and festivals of Advent, Christmas, New Year's and the Naming of Jesus, Epiphany, Transfiguration, Ash Wednesday, Lent, Holy Week (Passion/Palm Sunday, Maundy Thursday, Good Friday, Holy Saturday), Easter (including the Saturday-night Vigil), Ascension, Pentecost, Trinity Sunday, the weeks of Pentecost, Christ the King Sunday! Certainly we wouldn't take the gigantic gifts of Christmas for granted if we have spent four weeks of Advent preparing spiritually for Christ's past, present, and future comings (instead of getting bogged down in all the trappings and materialistic commodities, the endless activities and often empty arrangements). Surely we wouldn't miss the radical change that Easter ushers in if we have followed Jesus in all His sufferings for six weeks of Lent and have comprehended the depth of our sin which His passion annihilates and the coercive vigor of the principalities and powers over which His sacrifices triumph.

Such blessings of the LORD's name in worship

prepare us to witness to others. The more thoroughly our worship displays all the aspects of God's Triune covenant grace and mercy on our behalf, the more readily we will tell His glory to all the world.

IV What Will Be the Result of Genuine Worship?

> *Proclaim good tidings of His salvation from*
> *day to day.*
> *Tell of His glory among the nations,*
> *His wonderful deeds among all the peoples.*
>   PSALM 96:2b-3

One problem with separating the first three lines of Psalm 96 as we have is that we lose the thrust of the three lines together. Corporately they give a stirring call to praise that uses a literary device sometimes called "staircase parallelism" in that the repeated phrase "sing to the LORD" is expanded in different ways at each step.

Next, those first three lines are matched, in verses 2b-3, by another set of three lines. This second set begins with two parallel lines and then adds a staircase expansion to the object and indirect objects of the verbs in a third line. Furthermore, this whole initial set of six lines in Psalm 96 is matched in verses 7-9 with two comparable sets of three at the beginning and end of a nine-line expanded composition. The significance of this overall structure will be underscored when we discuss the second set of six. The poetic importance of these literary structures intensifies the psalm's revelations and what we can learn from them about worship.

Regarding the first set of six in Psalm 96, several scholars suggest that the first three lines should be translated as "Sing *of YHWH*" rather than "Sing *to YHWH*," as has been explicated above. If these commentators are right, then the first three lines match the significance of verses 2b-3, for then all six lines would refer to telling or singing about God for the sake of our neighbors. If the preposition is to be rendered "to," then there is a momentous progression between the two sets of three lines, moving from our growth as God's people by means of worship into our response as believers in proclaiming God's good news to the nations.

I couldn't underscore too much how crucial that sequence is, for many dissensions concerning worship arise because of our era's confusion between worship and evangelism, to the detriment of both. Many factors have led to this misunderstanding. One is the panic about declining numbers noted above. Another is the intensifying passivity of our cultural milieu, which causes some Christians to want to be entertained, rather than to do the work of worship. A third is related, for worship services are turned into a congregation's primary evangelistic tool because *the people* are not engaged in the practice of witnessing to their neighbors or in the difficulties of loving them.

Another reason for the confusion is historical. In the past, North America was thought to be a Christian society. In many local communities nearly everyone "went to church." With such a majority, believers never thought or talked about doing mission at home. "Missions" were done in exotic foreign lands, by people brave enough to face the pagans and live in austere conditions. There was no need to evangelize our neighbors.

Consequently, churches have failed for dozens of years to equip their members for daily mission. The problem is aggravated by inaccurate vocabulary—and if we speak bad theology, we live it.

In the United States today, the primary vocabulary is that we are "going to church." What horrible theology, for the phrase turns "church" into merely a building or one hour a week!

No! Instead let's recognize that we are going to a church building, a worship center, a sanctuary, a house of praise, or some other name for the place. There we are gathering with the community, the assembly, the saints, the congregation, the people of God for the purpose of worship, education, fellowship, or service. These practices will equip us to "Be Church" throughout the week—24 hours a day, 365 days a year.

If we spoke this way, then we would more often remember that we assemble for worship with God's people and that in worship the focus is on God. The result of worshiping will be that we know the Trinity better and will be formed to be more like Jesus by the power of the Holy Spirit. The more we are immersed in the good news of Christ's salvation, the more we will want to "proclaim [it] from day to day." We will be eager to "tell of His glory among the nations." We will know more of "His wonderful deeds" and will declare them "among all the peoples."

In speaking engagements I usually illustrate the difference between worship and evangelism by holding up a large school picture of my husband and describing him in detail as a teacher, a gardener, a gentle caregiver for me in my handicaps. That is the language of introduction spoken to those who don't know *about* Myron. It parallels the language of witness and evangelism in which I tell my neighbors *about* God to introduce them to Someone they haven't yet known.

But that is not the way I will talk *with* Myron when I get home from my speaking trip. Then I will speak the language of relationship, of adoration and growth, of devotion and commitment. That corresponds to worship, which is direct expression *to* God of praise and thanksgiving and intercession and *from* God through the Scriptures and various servants of the Word and through the Lord's Supper.

Now that we have separated evangelism and worship, let's connect them.

Worship and evangelism are inextricably intertwined, but the first is the goal and the second is the means. The work of worshiping God will form us to be bearers of God's love to our neighbors. We will become the kind of friends who will give witness to the world. I am convinced that if our churches would really "Be Church," our lives as individuals and our common life as a congregation would kindle in our neighbors a desire for such a relationship with God. In addition, if any

The work of worshiping God will form us to be bearers of God's love to our neighbors.

nonbelievers came to our worship services (though they couldn't technically "worship" since they wouldn't know God's worthiness) and if they observed

how joyfully and attentively we praise God and listen to His Word, they would probably be stirred and would want to learn more about this God and life. Our thankfulness, lament, confession, petitions and intercessions, and adoration could be quite convincing.

Furthermore, genuine corporate worship inevitably spreads out into giving witness to our neighbors. Psalm 96:2b-3 underscores that expansion by describing our testimony with several parallel phrases. It is essential to remind us (since this isn't evident in our English translations) that all the verbs are plural. We all—all the believers—are commanded to sing, bless, proclaim, and tell. Evangelism is not the work of the pastor, nor of the worship service. It is the task of every single Christian.

It is not an onerous burden, for it is not difficult to "proclaim" if the subject of our proclamation is "good tidings." I've never yet met a person who has just gotten engaged who tells me so without being exuberant. On a much larger scale, we have such great news to express about God's salvation (in all its fullness!) that we will be declaring it all the time, from day to day.

The first line of verse 3 adds two more dimensions to our witness, for it enjoins us to "tell of [YHWH's] glory among the nations." If our worship is filled with God's Splendor—in all kinds of sounds and songs, artworks, Scripture texts, homiletical insights, holy silences, corporate prayers, forgiveness and peace-filled blessings— then we'll have much to tell! And we will tell it to those who aren't acquainted with the Trinity. The Hebrew word translated "nations" is *goyim,* which the Israelites often used to signify the Gentiles, the heathen, those who didn't know God.

With a poetic parallel, the second line of verse 3 expands both the subject matter and the audience. Now we are urged to tell God's "wonderful deeds among *all* the peoples" (emphasis mine). We tell our neighbors and we also support those evangelists and missionaries proclaiming the Gospel in every land (or maybe we go to another mission field ourselves). And what we tell others is all the ways that God is working—all the fantastic, phenomenal, and unfathomed deeds of our amazing LORD. Worship is one place where we learn what those deeds are; that is why worship daren't be shallow, for it equips the saints with such a vision of God's glory and God's deeds that we can't help but tell the world.

There is also a place for specific evangelistic events, though that place is smaller than many Christians assume. If we look at Acts 2, as one example, we notice the major evangelistic sermon of Peter, which led (after further discussion with the disciples) to many persons coming to faith. Immediately, these new believers were immersed in the Christian way of life—continued, steadfast devotion to the apostles' doctrine, fellowship, the breaking of the (communion) bread, prayers, signs and wonders, economic redistribution, and worship (Acts 2:42-47). This way of life caused many more to be brought to faith. All three evangelistic means were part of the total witness: Peter's sermon, further discussion, and a way of life that made outsiders wonder, yearn for it, and, by God's grace, adopt it.

It is a major flaw in present-day churches that

we don't realize that our primary evangelistic tool is *the corporate life of the believing community*. Our neighbors need to see a Christian way of life that gives warrant for belief! Therefore, our worship should be rich with the splendors of God—to which we will give witness in daily life.

This understanding requires several major paradigm shifts, for our culture has severely misconstrued what it means to be the Church. A genuinely biblical understanding will be thoroughly countercultural in significant ways.

For example, in our culture, driven by consumerism, by each person choosing what he or she wants and likes, the prevailing paradigm is to choose a church for what suits you and meets your needs. The biblical picture instead is of a people who belong to a community of saints not by choice, but by proximity—which is still the notion in the Roman Catholic sense of "parish." The result of learning to live together with one's neighbors as brothers and sisters in the LORD was that the entire community was continually being formed for daily mission. If we are really going to be Church

> **Our worship should be rich with the splendors of God—to which we will give witness in daily life.**

for the sake of our neighbors in the twenty-first century, this reversal of our society's emphasis on choice is imperative.

We cannot merely attract our neighbors with entertaining "worship" events. It will require that we love them deeply, perhaps at great cost to ourselves, and that we be prepared to mentor them in discipleship since so many people in our age know nothing about God.

V What Idols Tempt Us Away from Worshiping the Only True God?

For great is the LORD, and greatly to be praised;
*   He is to be feared above all gods.*
For all the gods of the peoples are idols,
*   But the LORD made the heavens.*

PSALM 96:4-5

We can learn a great deal about worship by looking at the earliest Christians, for the culture that surrounded them was in many ways similar to ours in twenty-first-century North America. Then and now the population is highly pluralistic, with the people's "spirituality" being characterized by devotion to all kinds of gods. Many of the pagan religions of the first centuries A.D. are being resuscitated these days—and many of the earliest Christian heresies are, too, as some scholars and lay people deny the divinity of Christ or advocate goddess worship or tacitly renounce the importance of our roots in the Old Testament. Ancient nature worship is revived by those whose Sunday locations for adoration are the golf links or the hiking trails and ski slopes. Jesus recognized Mammon as one of the most powerful idolatries, and it still holds that position.

The early Christians were surrounded by allegiances to other gods, such as the pantheons of Roman and Greek deities and their incarnation in the Roman state. Similarly, today North America is flooded with religions from all over the world, and the idolatry of the nation-state leads to political abuses and economic oppressions by the superpower and ethnic cleansings by lesser powers.

We can tell from the Scriptures that the worship of the early Church exposed the reigning idolatries and dethroned them. The book of Revelation insists that Jesus Christ is LORD even though Caesar claimed that title. Paul gives specific directions for "desacralizing" or "dedivinizing" Mammon by gathering an offering when the saints assembled for worship. Other biblical texts depose particular religious leaders (even as the idolatry of charismatic personalities in pastors, worship leaders, or musicians needs to be renounced today) or emphasize that Christ crucified—and not human successes—must be the subject of preaching.

Resistance and Inoculation

Psalm 96:4-5 gives us excellent guidelines for resisting the idolatries that threaten our worship in the twenty-first century. Its second line also inoculates us with a vaccine that can build up antibodies to inhibit infectious idolatries from invading.

As we have seen above, worship is for God. It centers on recognizing that "great is the LORD, and greatly to be praised" and on responding to that worthiness by gathering with others to praise God as is His due. If the community—and each of us as individuals in that Body—focuses totally on the greatness of the LORD and His deserving to be praised, we will resist all idolatries of self and comfort and ease, all divinizing of worship leaders, all sacralizing of our tastes and preferences, all gods of power or success.

> Worship centers on recognizing that "great is the LORD, and greatly to be praised" and on responding to that worthiness by gathering with others to praise God as is His due.

One aspect of our faith that vaccinates us against idolatries is the biblical notion of fear, for the LORD is "to be feared above all gods." It seems to me that our postmodern times suffer from a lack of genuine "fear" for God. I put the word *fear* in quotation marks because its Old Testament usage does not signify "terror," nor does it connote simply awe and reverence. When biblical writers named the "fear of the Lord" that is "the beginning of wisdom" (especially in the Psalms and Proverbs), they identified a profound realization of our unworthiness before God so that we do not take God's gracious love and steadfast mercy for granted, as if we deserved it or could earn it or pay it back.

Our faith would build up more antibodies against idolatrous infections in our worship if we understood more clearly and kept in mind more strongly the scriptural tension of fear and love in our relationship with God. Too frequently in our post-Christian, tolerant world, we overemphasize one side or the other of that dialectical tension and thereby lose the compelling combination of the two that characterizes the Scriptures.

For example, throughout the Psalms the poets write about both the profound fear with which they have observed such aspects as the inevitability of death or the power of God's actions in nature and also the love with which they adore their covenant Lord. Similarly, the apostle Paul agonizes over his seemingly inescapable bondage to sin (Romans 7) just before exulting over the truth that Jesus Christ has delivered us and that nothing can separate us from the love of God demonstrated and fulfilled in Him (Romans 8).

We can hardly even begin to appreciate the amazing grace of God's love unless we first have known how much we definitely deserve instead our Judge's righteous wrath, how we incontrovertibly deserve the death we each must die. Without such proper "fear," we assume that it is easy (and merited) for God to forgive us. We nonchalantly think that we're not too bad—

> **W**e can hardly even begin to appreciate the amazing grace of God's love unless we first have known how much we definitely deserve instead our Judge's righteous wrath.

that we could actually earn God's favor. We make grace cheap.

When we totally confront our absolute hopelessness and complete depravity, however, we recognize with awe and trembling the nobility and immeasurability and incomprehensibility of God's love for us. God could at any moment ignore or destroy us; that is what we deserve. But the LORD does not; that is His grace. The Trinity's character is to remain faithful at all times, under all circumstances, to the divine covenant promises. Only with a constant intermingling of fear and love can we genuinely worship such a God.

Worship Idolatries

We need the vaccine of proper fear and love and a bolstered resistance to idolatries because "all the gods of the peoples are idols" (Psalm 96:5) and the gods of our culture constantly tend to invade our churches and worship services. Many of the fights churches have over worship questions are aggravated by the tendency to idolize certain positions. We've seen above the idolatry of "traditional" and "contemporary" which is often provoked by inadequate understanding of what the terms signify in the battle.

Closely related is our culture's idolatry of everything *new*, though in worship materials the new is often not sorted (as denominational hymnbooks as well as time already did with older music) so that the best of the contemporary genres can be used. On the opposite side, many sacralize the old, without noticing that some hymns and forms from bygone eras have lasted for terrible reasons (such as fatuous sentimentality).

We could make a long list of dialectical opposites which are both needed in worship, though sometimes partisans in worship conflicts advocate only one side or the other. Some prominent examples are these:

truth from God	response to God
head	heart
freshness	continuity with the past
contextualization	universality
new expressions	familiarity for the sake of participation
order	freedom in the Spirit
Joy, delight, elation	sorrow, penitence, lament
enthusiastic expression	silence
ritual	spontaneity
simplicity	complexity

Many of the idolatries in churches stem from our society's consumerism. Some people come to worship in order to be entertained or to be made to feel good, to be comfortable, rather than to engage actively in worshiping God (which should sometimes make us experience anything but comfort!). Closely related is the expectation that the worship leaders or preacher will offer us a good

performance, instead of serve as stage managers
who help all of us offer our best performance to
God, who is the audience of our worship. Also
correlatively, some churches resort to gimmicks
or techniques, instead of relying on the truth of
God's Word and the power of the Holy Spirit.

Our culture's idolatry of appearances often invades a church in such forms as these: inordinate
attention paid to the leaders' looks, makeup and
clothes; the professionalism of the worship
"show"; the luxuriousness of the church building or of its furnishings or artworks or musical instruments; the size of the worshiping community
or the speed with which the numbers of worshipers increase; the frequency with which a congregation surpasses its neighbors in attendance
(often by means of "sheep stealing" or "expan-
sionism instead of mission"[8]); the recognition of
its success by the larger public community or the
denomination; the extent of its programs; the diversity of its worship choices; the degree to
which the most current technology is used; the
popularity of its televised services; the prestige
gained by those who worship there; the fun to be
enjoyed in the worship service. All these
sacralizations demonstrate the common problem,

masterfully verbalized by George Hunsberger, that the congregations function as "vendors of religious services and goods," instead of as "a body of people sent on a mission."[9]

We can hardly escape being idolatrous, for our society has formed us with a consumer mentality. We spend our lives choosing what pleases us, so it is decidedly countercultural to search instead for what pleases God. That is why it is critically important that our churches not foster such a church shopping disposition by offering choices of different kinds of worship services. Can we learn instead to be a Body of diverse people, learning from each other's music how to praise God more fully? Can we discover from the early Church the reasons it developed worship as it did, even as we constantly learn from new expressions of faith? Can we cease using power plays by which we expose and defeat other idolatries in order to hide our own?

The practice of combating idolatries for the sake of genuine worship also equips the members of our churches for resisting the idolatries they encounter in daily life. In a culture awash in sacralizations of money, power, prestige, possessions, technology, toys, sexual "freedom," and

The practice of combating idolatries for the sake of genuine worship also equips the members of our churches for resisting the idolatries they encounter in daily life. self, Christians completely require the LORD's greatness to withstand, abstain from, and counter them.

The Scriptures we read in worship continue to *expose* these gods by publicly displaying them; the sermons of the preacher can equip parishioners to *disarm* them; the power of the Holy Spirit with which worship fills us enables us to *triumph* over them. (These three verbs come from the pattern of Christ's victory over the principalities and powers as described in Colossians 2.) Other elements of the worship service provide other forms of conquest over the powers of idolatry. Giving a monetary offering, for example, continually defeats Mammon.

God Has Triumphed over All Other Gods

It is important to conclude this section on idolatries with a thorough recognition of how utterly God has triumphed over all the world's divinizations. Psalm 96:5b hints at the first dimension by proclaiming that "the LORD made the heavens." Our first means for defeating idols is to recognize their nonexistence. The only one capable of being GOD is the covenant, creator LORD. Other gods may demand our notice, but they are simply things, ideas, ideologies, technological devices, worldly powers, lies. Only one LORD has created the cosmos. Only One, revealed as Triune, deserves our praise and adoration.

Secondly, Jesus Christ has totally vanquished all principalities and powers, all lords and gods in His thorough work of redemption. The last enemy to be defeated, death, was conquered at the empty tomb. The gods of Mammon, politics, religious power, misguided institutions, and all the idolatries of selfish ambitions were exposed in Christ's whole life of suffering and passion, compassion and death.

Thirdly, the Holy Spirit empowers us to annihilate idolatries. We have been given the belt of truth with which to stand against all powers. Other weapons in the panoply of God's armor (Ephesians 6) give us all that we need to defeat the gods that threaten the churches' worship and our daily lives. Will our worship services equip us with this sense of authority and with a heartfelt commitment to fulfilling God's call to us to overcome, overpower, and overthrow all idolatries?

VI | What Does God's Creation Have to Say about Worship?

But the LORD made the heavens.

PSALM 96:5b

The psalmist's declaration about the covenant *YHWH*'s creation of the cosmos indirectly invites us into two important considerations for those who lead worship. In contrast to the idols which we have just considered, which are characterized by their lies, the LORD's creation is constituted by truth. That is, all creation is congruent—its form matches its function; its parts cohere with the whole. This provides an excellent guideline for how we prepare and conduct worship.

I can illustrate this principle best with a good example of a bad example. Once when I was preaching in a Canadian church, the worship planners chose to use my hymn, "Come Away from Rush and Hurry," which is sung to the melody, "Beach Spring." Here is the first verse of this song:

Come away from rush and hurry
    to the stillness of God's peace;
From our vain ambition's worry,
    come to God to find release.
Come away from noise and clamor,
    Life's demands and frenzied pace;
Come to join the people gathered
    here to seek and find God's face.

Can you imagine that text being sung accompanied by pounding drums? The forceful hammer of a sharply percussive snare did not allow the worshipers to "come away from rush and hurry" to stillness and peace, to "come away from noise and clamor" and a "frenzied pace."

I was, I confess, a bit angry about it. The incoherence of the way the music was played compared with the text robbed worshipers of its message, for the true significance of what they experienced was that it is impossible to escape "rush and hurry, . . . noise and clamor."

In the second service I volunteered to accompany that song and encouraged the band to sit and participate in it instead. I played the melody on the piano as gently as I could and with as spare an accompaniment as possible.

After the congregation sang the hymn's three

verses, a long period of silence followed. Then a woman asked, "Could we please sing that again?" I asked the community if that would be their consensus, and the worshipers answered "Yes." They were thirsty for God's peace, for such a coming away from rush and hurry.

This illustration does not say that we should never use drums, nor is the subject the relative merits of this particular song. My point is simply the importance of coherence and congruence. What we say in our hymns should be matched by how they sound. To praise God's majesty requires a regal pace; to sing of Christ's passion and death necessitates lament; rejoicing with Latino folk songs will be augmented by rhythm instruments; African-American spirituals ought to be sung in a way that remembers their origin in suffering.

> **W**hat we say in our hymns should be matched by how they sound.

A second major lesson for worship leaders from Psalm 96:5b is raised because the psalmist calls God by the covenant name, *YHWH,* as the Creator. This suggests relationship in the creating. The heavens are made by One whose character is steadfast love and faithfulness.

The creations of all those who lead worship should be undergirded with the same kind of character. We don't offer gifts of music or preaching or prayers or whatever else to perform or elevate ourselves. Our songs and sermons and intercessions are offered to adore God and for the spiritual well-being, the edification, of all who worship, and those gifts flow from the LORD's steadfast love and faithfulness surging through us. Consequently, even as the created heavens give glory to God, so our offerings of leadership are intended to enable the entire participating Body to glorify Him more thoroughly.

Two other lessons can also be drawn from the psalmist's comment about the LORD's creation. The first is that we hope as many congregation members as possible will contribute their creations to our worship. Can we encourage children to contribute their artworks (perhaps as bulletin covers or banners or flower arrangements)? Can we involve many of the youth in playing their musical instruments, singing in choirs, chiming bells, or chanting psalms? Could church members cast the pottery used to hold the communion bread, grow the flowers, sculpt a crucifix, carve an altar, needlepoint a kneeling cushion, design the vestments? Could entire families participate in the ushering, handle the sound equipment, present a chancel drama, teach the congregation new global music?

At one stunning church building in Pennsylvania, a senior citizens' needlepoint group made cushions for the kneelers at every pew in the sanctuary and at the communion rail, and all together their cushions exhibit the major symbols for every season of the entire church year. At a congregation in the Midwest, each worship service utilizes an orchestra made up of young and old together, with a wide variety of instruments. How can our churches' worship services call forth more of the gifts of the participants in the assembly?

My final point in this section arises because we are being overwhelmed in our culture by technology, which tends to replace "practices" that "engage" us with "devices" that simply produce "commodities."[10] There is a deep difference between buying the device of a backup tape to produce the commodity of musical accompaniment, on the one hand, and, on the other, training our children (and ourselves) to make music that engages us all in offering praise to God. The former is the production of a recording company; the latter is the sacrifice of our praise as worshipers. One is technology; the other is creation.

VII Do We Have a Big Enough God?

Splendor and majesty are before Him,
Strength and beauty are in His sanctuary.

PSALM 96:6

Part of my concern over how we use technological devices in our worship arises because the nature of our increasingly pervasive technological world has been to displace God. The first great scientists of the Enlightenment supposedly were believers (at least they used religious language) who thought that God wanted them to employ their inquiring minds and that their scientific projects would enable themselves and others better to understand God's creation. Similarly, advanced modern technology in general was first developed primarily with compassion to ease the burdens of humanity, to promote health and well-being. But now in the twenty-first century, many scientists seem to be playing God as such developments as the abortion pill and the human genome and cloning projects are celebrated with inadequate moral questioning. Similarly, technology in North America has violated the intricate balances of God's creation, but in response our culture has developed the attitude that human beings can solve

Part of my concern over how we use technological devices in our worship arises because the nature of our increasingly pervasive technological world has been to displace God.

all our problems if we just find the right "quickfix" technique—so who needs God anymore? For example, we've sought to counteract the "acts of God" in storms by developing technology to prevent and control floods (which are caused sometimes because we've built too much on nature's wetlands and sometimes by flood control devices further upstream).

Bill Gates, genius of Microsoft and the richest man on the globe, has publicly claimed that religion is "not very efficient" and that he has much better things to do on Sunday mornings. Many who idolize the technological milieu are too busy to bother with God. To "attend worship" on Sunday mornings would be to do God a favor.

Some churches rightfully wonder how to

evangelize such people, and many of them utilize technological wizardry to attract such folks. The focus then becomes not so much to display the glory of God as to delight the people who come.

You might think I am just a Luddite, afraid of the technological revolution and whining about it, but my intent here is more to provoke the readers of this book into asking better questions. For example, let's ask about every device we use in worship whether it causes worshipers to become more engaged in the actual physical/mental/spiritual work of worshiping God. Even more important, do our technological spectacles display the LORD's "splendor and majesty" or our own idolatry of contemporaneity or technology? Do we trust the Holy Spirit's power to change the hearts and lives of worship participants, or do we trust our own leadership skills and ardor or our dazzling multimedia techniques to convince? Is it better to utilize the devices of the technological milieu in worship to evangelize, or should our evangelism concentrate more on personal conversations in which we enable people to see both the dangers of their technological enthrallment and also the genuine "splendor and majesty" of the only true God? We've already considered above in section IV the detriment to both when worship and evangelism are confused.

To me it seems dangerous to think that our worship should be filled with all sorts of special effects in order to be "relevant" to young people in this new millennium. In *Books and Culture,* Tony Jones points out the peril as follows:

> As virtual reality becomes less virtual and more real, more and more people—especially youth—will choose this kind of ignorance: a life lived inside movies and games rather than in families and schools and relationships and jobs. Thankfully, we follow a Lord whose life and words 'invade our real world with a reality even more real than it is.' Our teens need that reality. So does our world.[11]

Similarly, the authors of the book *The Godbearing Life: The Art of Soul Tending for Youth Ministry* insist that adolescents have had enough of "simulations of transcendence."[12] Other scholars note that some young people are turning to Orthodoxy as they search for genuine transcendence, mystery, and roots in faith. From conversations with teenagers and people in their twenties and thirties, I'm convinced that they don't need more screens; they need relationships with real, really committed Christians who faithfully live the way of Jesus.

How best, then, can we display in our worship the "Splendor and majesty [which] are before Him"? Young people these days have lost their wonder. How can worship be of interest to them if they are usually dazzled by the scintillating glitz and electrifying energy of the fantastic phenomena in their multimedia world? If *exciting* and *awesome* are their favorite words to describe their milieu, won't the LORD we worship be boring?

Psalm 96:6a gives us some suggestions. We do not have to manufacture something interesting in God; we simply will, in worship, express and reflect who God really is! When we think of God's splendor, for example, in Christ's transfiguration in Matthew 17:1-8; Mark 9:1-8; Luke 9:28-36—or as that is revealed in every other Scripture text and in the Body of worshiping people with all their gifts—we realize that it

> **W**e do not have to manufacture something interesting in God; we simply will, in worship, express and reflect who God really is!

is brilliance without banality. God's splendor has distinction, but it is not domineering. It exhibits excellence that encourages our own. It is honorable in a way that calls forth reverence. The luster of God's splendor is not just a surface patina, but a radiance that remained, for example, even when Jesus was suffering the most horrible of deaths. The splendor of His compassion, in the midst of His agony, especially as recorded in Luke 23:33-49 and John 19:23-27, is utterly stunning.

Similarly, the psalm's term *majesty* hints at the uniqueness of the Trinity. Triune majesty is grand without being grandiose, preeminent without being prejudicial, impressive without being imperious, noble but not forcing us to notice.

The simple fact is this: God is GOD, and that is enough to claim our interest. If our worship services present God truly, there is no need to manufacture glitz. The substance of God is sufficiently inspiring. The basic fact of our human existence is that we long for God, even if—and perhaps especially if—we don't know it. Let us ask, then, whether each thing we do in worship truly presents the real Triune God.

Dialectical Opposites

Not only is God infinitely interesting and stunningly inconceivable, but He also contains many opposites within Himself. Though scholars differ in their interpretation of the second line of Psalm 96:6—with some treating the two terms as synonymous and others seeing them as more complementary—it seems to me that it would deepen our worship if we recognized the contrast of the "Strength and beauty [that] are in His sanctuary." Oftentimes what is strong is not beautiful, and what is beautiful might be fragile. Strength is sometimes destructive of beauty, and beauty might disarm strength and render it powerless.

God incomprehensibly contains within Himself many dialectical opposites, such as strength and beauty, wrath and love, power and tenderness, vulnerability and sovereignty. Worship can be endlessly exhilarating and thought-provok-

> **G**od incomprehensibly contains within Himself many dialectical opposites, such as strength and beauty.

ing because we will never get done exploring all there is to discover about God's disparate dimensions.

Because God's nature is so expansive as to encompass opposite poles, we who are formed in His image will best worship Him in similar dialectics. In section V above we considered the dialectic of our response to God in the combination of fear and love, and in section I we recognized that to be faithful in worship requires the dialectic that Jesus described as "spirit and truth." We have also considered the importance of using both new and old music, of being both rooted in the Church's past as well as constantly reforming our faith.

Because I increasingly focus on the urgency of bringing together opposing poles in the Christian life, I am disturbed by many new views of worship that emphasize one aspect at the expense of its balancing counterpart. This has always been a danger throughout the history of worship (with various strands accentuating opposing elements), but it is particularly evident today in worship movements which often ignore or even belittle the historic worship forms.

For example, some movements accentuate the *contextual* nature of worship, which is indeed important, but meanwhile devalue or dismiss what is *classical*.[13] In contrast, in the New Testament the first Christians used classical materials from Jewish synagogue and Temple worship, as well as elements of their new situation as Christians. Similarly, devoted missionaries entering a new field bring the faith as it has been expressed in many cultures throughout space and time, and gradually new songs and forms are developed appropriate to the particular context in which they work. No one can ever be immediately contextual, for the language of faith is never newly discovered. Always it builds on continuities from the past and the wisdom of our forebears, even as it is always expanding and becoming ever new.

While teaching in Madagascar several years ago, I was amazed at the beauty of the singing in worship services. Oftentimes the music would be harmonized in six to eight parts, with the words all sung for memory—and they were singing old Norwegian hymns! We also heard many new Malagasy songs. It was the best of classical and contextual together.

To be biblical, worship must let the classical faith (already wrestled through) constantly question the contextual to keep it rooted in the Church. If worship is only contextual or utilizes only new songs, then the Gospel's uniqueness is easily lost in cultural trappings, and it is more difficult to form Christians who live any differently from their neighbors. As one wise sage has observed, the church that marries the spirit of this age will be a widow in the next.

On the other hand, the contextual perpetually probes the classical to keep it really biblical and not merely sentimentally traditionalistic (rather than traditional). We must keep in mind Jaroslav Pelikan's famous distinction between good tradition, which is "the living faith of the dead," and destructive traditionalism, which is "the dead faith of the living."

It is tragic that somehow in the past centuries the word *liturgy* has gotten a bad name, since every worship service has one! Churches claim to be "non-liturgical," but actually there is no such thing, since the term *liturgy* (from the Greek *leitourgia*) literally means "the work of the people." I hope every congregation involves the people in worship; without liturgical participation, one or a group of leaders is merely putting on a show to entertain. Moreover, every worship service follows some kind of ordering (even those given to charismatic expression in which a typical pattern becomes predictable), and this ordering makes it possible for those present truly to become engaged in active worshiping. Liturgy is the vehicle enabling all to participate thoroughly.

Sometimes critics contrast liturgy with liberty, but actually the two go hand in hand. Liberty prevents liturgy from becoming stuck in ruts, but liturgy prevents liberty from being abused or from becoming abusive. Paul had to write several chapters in 1 Corinthians because the church at Corinth took too much "liberty" in worship and caused offense to the poor (chapter 11), to members whose gifts were degraded or rejected (12), to those who were not genuinely loved (13), to strangers who were not edified (14). Some members even took liberty with doctrine and denied the resurrection (15). Liberty is not necessarily a good thing.

C. S. Lewis expressed better than anyone the true liberty of liturgy in this analogy:

> Novelty, simply as such, can have only an enter-
> tainment value. And [believers] don't go to
> church to be entertained. They go to *use* the
> service, or, if you prefer, to *enact* it. Every ser-
> vice is a structure of acts and words through
> which we receive a sacrament, or repent, or

supplicate, or adore. And it enables us to do these things best—if you like, it "works" best—when, through long familiarity, we don't have to think about it. As long as you notice, and have to count, the steps, you are not yet dancing but only learning to dance. A good shoe is a shoe you don't notice. Good reading becomes possible when you need not consciously think about eyes, or light, or print, or spelling. The perfect church service would be one we were almost unaware of; our attention would have been on God.[14]

Against Lewis's dancing analogy, those who reject "liturgical worship" claim that worship is boring if the same forms are used week after week. It is true that many churches get lazy and rigidly follow a hymnbook or prayerbook order of worship without any variation whatsoever. However, well-planned liturgies will include many changes for the seasons of the church year and weekly differences in prayers, Scripture lessons, Psalms, and responses.

The rigidity of some churches using historic liturgies and the abuse of liberty in some churches which reject it both demonstrate the need for maintaining a dialectical tension between these two poles. Then worship will be sustained by a liturgical structure (which can utilize many styles and forms) that genuinely liberates worshipers to concentrate on God without being distracted by either novelty or monotony. The goal, in Lewis's image, is to be able truly to dance, without having to count steps—i.e., freely to experience God and to express our responses with the whole community.

Ancient liturgies, used in Orthodox, Roman Catholic, Anglican, and Lutheran churches primarily, were first developed so that everyone could participate and so that their involvement taught them many texts from the Scriptures. Long before I could read as a child, I could be fully engrossed in the worship services because I knew the catholic (that is, universal) liturgy for memory. Liturgical phrases and elements used week after week actually enable non-readers, the visually impaired, and young children to participate much more fully than do most free-form services because they can be involved in songs and sentences known by heart.

Liturgy is criticized for turning worship into an empty, rote "performance," but that happens in services called "non-liturgical," too. It is also true that some organists and song leaders, some choirs and worship bands perform concerts instead of enabling all the people to worship more thoroughly. Worship should never be the performance of a few trained people.

Instead it is the performance of every one, the active participation of each. If we forget that worship is for God or if we give in to the idolatry of comfort, we won't work very hard at being thoroughly involved if we don't feel like it. Contrarily, if we remember that public worship presents the opportunity to unite with others in gratitude to the King of the cosmos, we will each want to do our best and offer our most excellent singing—our finest *performance*—and join with all the other saints in thorough *participation* in the act of worship.

My point is not to argue for any specific kind of liturgy, but to recognize liturgy and liberty as partners in helping all the worshipers participate as fully as possible and perform to the best of their ability for God, our audience. Such an understanding of performance is suggested in a psalm verse that parallels the beginning of Psalm 96. Verse 3 of Psalm 33 commands, "Sing to Him a new song; Play *skillfully* with a shout of Joy!" I italicize *skillfully* and capitalize *Joy* because if we fully enter into praising the LORD and offer our adoration as skillfully, excellently, and whole-heartedly as we can, it will increase our heavenly Joy. The more we invest ourselves and our wills in discovering and lauding the glory of God, the more we will be filled with the bliss of His Triune presence.

I want to restore this positive sense of the word *performance* because of an astonishing encounter several years ago when I urged a woman with an excellent alto voice to sing in the choir I directed. (In directing both choirs and folk teams I've always emphasized that their primary purpose is to help the rest of the congregation sing better.) She answered that she would rather sing in the folk team because then she wouldn't have to pay attention to breathing and phrasing and such things. Do folk team members not pay attention to phrasing, for the sake of making sense of their praise? Do they not offer their best vocal tones so that their gift of worship to God is as excellent as possible? If so, then breathing matters, too. And if we are not in a choir or folk team, do we not still sing our best as our sacrifice of praise?

When we construct worship services, we must always remember that it is *public* worship for which we are concerned. Thus, we keep asking how we can enable perfect strangers to participate. If church members enter into a cozy little domain, a private *tête-à-tête* (or "head to head") with God, then how will someone who doesn't know how to worship become involved? Liturgical prayers new or old not only allow someone not familiar with the congregation to join in the prayers of that group of people, they also enable them to participate with the Church throughout space and time by means of one of the Church's communal prayers.

How can liturgical forms be assets, rather than obstructions, in encountering God? We can better understand how if we remember that no one can really enter into an "immediate" relationship with God. Even as Jesus gives us access to His Father, so the Church's gift of "ritual" enables us truly to receive His gifts. Liturgical scholar James White teaches that "ritual" is the means by which God's self-giving presence is conveyed to worship participants.

Though the word *ritual* is rejected by many in our culture, the fact that people without religion develop alternate rituals (for New Year's Eve, the Super Bowl, birthdays, and weddings, for example) demonstrates how the human psyche needs such ordering. Little children get upset if their usual bedtime ritual is modified or forgotten.

What should be rejected is not ritual itself, but *false* ritual—gestures that are overstated or performed without honesty or meaning, rites which have lost their theocentric (i.e., God-centered) focus, ceremonies which are merely formal without genuine honor or reverence for God. True ritual keeps us mindful of God and of the great privilege of worshiping Him. (Have you noticed this book's "ritual" that the words *He*, *Him*, and *His* are capitalized when they refer to God, though in most books and Bibles that practice has been abandoned? Has that gesture helped you hallow God's name and be more conscious of the LORD's exaltation?)

Whatever liturgy our church uses, may it enable the ritual of our public worship to point to God, to encourage everyone's participation, and to knit us together as a believing community. May the liturgy liberate us to dance our praise because we are mindful not of the steps, but of

God. And may that liberty cause us more deeply to understand the liturgy's meaning.

The importance of liturgical participation and ritual raises other dialectical issues. Some present-day worship movements claim that worship should be celebrative and not cerebral, full of intimacy rather than awe. Biblical worship includes all of those. Extraordinarily celebrative psalms, for example, are always based on cerebral recognition of reasons for which God is praised. True festivity must always include some intellectual consciousness or else it degenerates into shallow hype.

When in daily life we celebrate someone's birthday, the festivity is more deeply meaningful if we let the occasion remind us of the birthday person's gifts to the world and of the gifts of life that have been given to that individual. Similarly, the dinner party my husband and I hosted last night was richer because we consciously prepared the table, the meal, and ourselves for our company and their conversation—and afterwards, as we washed the dishes, we reflected on the many gifts of the evening. In that way, the festivity lasted many more hours—both before and after the actual party when our guests were present—because we cerebrally relished the celebration.

Worship that emphasizes only celebration highlights only one dimension of biblical faith. We also need to worship with lament, confession, our doubts and frustrations, and life's pains and sorrows so that our vocabulary for God displays God's presence in every aspect of our lives.

Moreover, genuine renewal requires continual development of the mind of faith (especially in our culture of mindlessness). Notice, for example, how in Romans 12:2 Paul encourages us literally to *"be being transformed* by the renewal of your mind" (my translation). The continuing and passive verb in the original Greek of that verse accents God's constant work to transform us and renew our minds.

Then mindfulness leads to mission. Mission moves in wrong directions, mimicking the issues of the culture, unless it is thoroughly grounded in biblical study and prayer to envision God's larger plan for the world. On the other hand, meditation becomes escapist if it doesn't lead to celebrative mission. The faithful life continually swings between both contemplative and activist poles in order to be meditatively missional and mission-minded when we meditate.

Similarly awe of God and intimacy with God

nourish each other. Many of the Psalms both praise the LORD personally for His wondrous deeds, and also acknowledge His authority over the whole earth and the awesome power of His Word. Psalm 33 provides a good model.

The psalm begins with a call to the "righteous ones" to "sing for joy *in* the LORD" using various instruments. The first 5 verses of the psalm praise *YHWH* for His upright word, that His works are done in faithfulness, that He loves righteousness and justice, that the earth is full of His lovingkindness. Then the poem shifts in verses 6-18a to concentrate more on God's power and our response of reverence and fear. The strophes describe creation, the LORD's nullifying of the counsel of nations, His observation of all humankind; in response, "all the inhabitants of the world" are commanded to "stand in awe of Him" (8b). The dialectical interplay of both fear/awe and love/intimacy is reinforced by the larger range of our responses to God in these last verses of Psalm 33:

Behold, the eye of the LORD is on those who fear Him,
*   On those who hope for His lovingkindness,*
To deliver their soul from death,
*   And to keep them alive in famine.*

Our soul waits for the LORD;
He is our help and our shield.
For our heart rejoices in Him,
Because we trust in His holy name.
Let Thy lovingkindness, O LORD, be upon us,
According as we have hoped in Thee. (verses 18-22)

Notice that the poet is both cerebral and celebrative, responding to God with fear and love, rejoicing and trust, waiting and hope. Our worship ought not to concentrate on one to the exclusion of the other, but can encompass the whole range of human emotions and will, of mind and heart, of being and action, of praycrfulness.

Without foundation in both sides of various dialectics, Christians' "intimacy with God" can easily be a false one—merely cozy feelings or an insidiously deceitful conception of God. The Bible demonstrates that genuine intimacy with God involves wrestling (e.g., Jacob in Genesis 32:24-32), persecution (Paul in 2 Timothy 3:12), even fear (the disciples in Mark 10:32-34). Intimacy with our Lord Jesus Christ is lived out in "the fellowship of His sufferings" (see especially Philippians 3:7-11 and 2 Corinthians 4:7-11). Such faith holds all the poles of fear/love, intimacy/awe, and celebration/mindfulness in dialectical tension, with both sides being fruitfully deepened.

Liturgical ordering includes all these dialectics. Scripture texts call us to mindfulness and also give direction for specific mission. Hymns and songs might be contemplative or might encourage and celebrate particular mission. Meditational prayer comes from both intimacy and awe and includes the mission of the Church throughout the world and the particular missions of our local congregation and its individual members.

Maintaining all these facets of our relationship with God is a never-ending process. That is why many of the manuals for how to do worship in the present age are dangerous, for they frequently prescribe "successful" strategies that do not consider the local situation in which worship is conducted and the sides of various dialectical sets which perhaps have been overly accentuated. No liturgical scholar, theologian, or sociologist can designate how worship should be conducted in a particular place. Rather, each congregation must ask better questions, so that in every place our worship is faithful to the kind of God we have and the biblical guidance He has condescended to give us. Does your church have a big enough God?

Musical Dialectics

Because worship expresses many dialectical combinations in God's character and in our responses to God, we need a wide variety of instruments and musical sounds to express them. Lamentably, many new worship movements are very critical of organs, while other churches use them exclusively.

Contemporary hostility towards pipe organs perhaps arose because some organists played them overbearingly or for their own glory, because some instruments are too large for their space and overwhelm the singers, or because some musicians do not know which stops to use to best support congregational singing. Idolatrous advocacy of organs forgets that they became the primary instruments for worship simply because one musician could play so many different kinds of sounds and not because it has greater endorsement from God. For whatever reasons, it is tragic that such a versatile instrument generates such animosity. Most well-built pipe organs, if played well, can sound like strings, brass, woodwinds, or an entire orchestra with a few simple stop changes and thereby display many different dimensions of God.

On the other hand, much of the dislike of worship bands arises if the instrumentation is always the same or if the band attempts to display certain attributes of God, such as splendor or magnificence, simply by cranking up amplifiers to higher decibel levels. Some of God's qualities can be better revealed by means of instruments with fuller sounds or can be achieved by involving more members of the congregation utilizing a larger diversity of instruments. The whimsy of God could be played with a pennywhistle, but God's royalty needs a trumpet.

Percussionists sometimes use the same rhythms and patterns endlessly repeated without much attention to how those sounds match the meaning of the words being sung. Being able to predict precisely when the drummer will roll the cymbal eliminates any surprise of sound to teach us something

Some of God's qualities can be better revealed by means of instruments with fuller sounds or can be achieved by involving more members of the congregation utilizing a larger diversity of instruments.

new about God. (In contrast, I remember once experiencing a shock of Joy when a timpani suddenly rolled at the climax of a hymn of praise.)

Percussion in worship is often limited to a trap
set featuring snare drums, which are too sharply
percussive (unless played with soft mallets) for
the human ear. Snares were invented to be heard
on the battlefield above the roar of muskets. They
produce a piercing sound that causes the ear to
close up in self-defense. The result is that singers
don't really hear each other—and, in turn, they
usually sing less. Perhaps we could instead produce our percussion by involving more people
playing a few octaves of bells or bell trees, African rain sticks or drum boxes with varied
pitches, Conga drums or African rattles, Orff
rhythm instruments, clavés or a casaba, a Latin
American guiro or maracas, or the organ's
zimbelstern (somewhat like the Christmas decora-
tion in which lighted candles cause air currents
that move little angels to spin and strike chimes).

As a frequent guest preacher in worship services in various denominations and locations, I
have noticed that people are often rendered passive if snare drums are too sharp for their ears,
and then they watch worship instead of partici-

pating in the singing. At one parish before worship began, I commented to the drummer (as he carried out piece after piece of his trap set) that the volume would make me plug my ears since one is deaf so I protect the other from loud or piercing sounds. He responded, "Lots of people plug their ears." Is this helpful for their worship? Shouldn't a percussionist be concerned if his playing is preventing the people's participation in worship rather than assisting it?

In a culture in which our musical tastes tend to get narrowed by the bombast of music produced to market, could not the sounds of worship expand our experience? Could we not better demonstrate the greatness of God with more varied sounds? Don't we need different kinds of sounds according to the seasons of the church year, according to whether we are confessing our sins or rejoicing in God's forgiveness or preparing to re-enter the world for mission? Sometimes we need simple unaccompanied singing; sometimes we need holy silence to contemplate God. At the very large St. Mark's Episcopal Cathedral near the University

Could we not better demonstrate the greatness of God with more varied sounds?

of Washington in Seattle, Sunday evening compline services (compline is the final service of the ancient monasteries' "hours") are packed every week with mostly young adults; they sit on the floor and against the walls when the pews are full—and they come for worship led by a men-and-boy's choir singing unaccompanied chant.

Whatever musical accompaniment we use must always be faithful to the character of the LORD and glorifying to God, congruent with the text it accompanies, and enabling worshipers to participate more fully. Organists in the past dedicated their entire lives to play their instruments well for the glory of God. They spent many years learning to play appropriately and many hours practicing for each worship service. Is that same sort of devotion demonstrated by all those who offer their musical gifts today (with whatever instruments or voices) to facilitate and enhance the congregation's worship?

VIII How Has the Church Developed Its Ascribing?

Ascribe to the LORD, O families of the peoples,
  Ascribe to the LORD glory and strength.
Ascribe to the LORD the glory of His name;

PSALM 96:7-8a

As pointed out in our discussion of the first six lines of Psalm 96, here again in verses 7-9 the poet constructed two sets of three lines —the first set of which calls us to worship and the second which describes how we respond.

The call to praise is similar in many ways to verses 1-2a, though the ordering is not exactly similar. In both places a greater group than just ourselves is called to praise—here "families of the peoples" and there "all the earth." These two phrases remind us that our local churches never worship by themselves, but are part of all the peoples everywhere and all the creaturely inhabitants of the earth who respond to their Creator.

Both sets of three lines calling to praise accentuate God's name—in verse 2a that we should "bless His name" and in 8a that we should "ascribe to the LORD the glory *of* His name." The implication of both is that God's character is too wonderfully multifarious and magnificent to be captured simply. There is always need for more singing, more ascribing (the true meaning of the word *praise*).

It is important, therefore, that we recognize that the Church throughout time and space has developed various patterns to "ascribe to the LORD glory and strength." Do these have a basic structure? What major divergences from the primary structures have appeared in history?

The Church's Development of Worship

The earliest Christians took some of their patterns for worship from the Jewish synagogue services, including prayers and readings from the Scriptures, though the evidence concerning the exact forms is scanty. One main difference between Jewish and Christian worship was the celebration of the Lord's Supper as the high point of the latter. However, the *Didache* or *Teaching of the Twelve Apostles,* which was perhaps begun around the time the Apostle Paul was writing and which developed to its final form by the end of the first century A.D., indicates that the great prayer of thanksgiving said by Christians at the Lord's Supper followed patterns from Jewish ritual meals.

Though in the first centuries of the Church worship developed differently in various places around the Mediterranean (with its early centers of Christianity such as Jerusalem, Alexandria, Rome, and Constantinople), local churches would have understood themselves as part of the "one, holy, catholic, apostolic Church" which is confessed in the Nicene Creed (originating in the Council of Nicaea called by Constantine in 325 A.D.). Though there were always differences in doctrine and practice along with the ebb and flow of various heresies, towards the end of the first millennium A.D. the unified Church moved more and more towards a monumental division between Eastern and Western Christianity, between Orthodox and Roman Catholic churches. Such worship practices as whether or not to employ icons were part of the numerous reasons for the separation.

Many more splits in the Church took place in the Age of Reformation with the development of

Lutheranism in Germany and Scandinavia, Anglicanism in England, and Reformed churches centered in Calvin's Geneva. Though these churches highlighted various aspects of doctrine, worship in western Europe (with the exception of the Reformed churches) generally paralleled that of Roman Catholicism. It is helpful to recognize that this fourfold structure seems to have pervaded most expressions of Christian worship from biblical times: Gathering, Word, Meal, Sending.[15] Most liturgies of most Christian churches basically follow that pattern, with more or less elaboration of the various parts.

Over the course of its first few centuries, the catholic (universal) Church amplified this pattern in a wonderful progression of elements that taught the major elements of Christian doctrine. Worshipers participated in liturgical responses that were taken directly from the Scriptures, especially from the Psalms and from the songs in Luke and Revelation. Later in history numerous composers set the major parts of "the Mass" in glorious arrangements using various combinations of choirs, congregation, organs, and orchestras.

Many people who grew up in so-called "liturgical" churches take the logical progression of the historic liturgy for granted or have never really been taught why various amplifications of the fourfold pattern have come into use. In contrast, some who grew up in supposedly "non-liturgical" churches have been taught a prejudice against the larger Church's heritage and consequently never discover what our forebears in worship can teach us. It is far better for both groups if we can remember that we all have "liturgies" and if we can learn why our churches use whatever elements they do from the Scriptures and the patterns of the larger Church.

A few years ago I was asked to lead a sectional on the historic liturgy at a worship conference sponsored by Western (Baptist) Seminary in Portland, Oregon, and I honestly didn't think many registrants at the gathering would be interested. To my great surprise, the room was packed; to my greater delight, many of the participants commented that they hoped to incorporate more of the elements from the heritage in their own churches' Gathering, Word, Meal, and Sending segments.

Similarly, often when I explain the importance in a worship service of confession and absolution (forgiveness), many people whose churches' liturgies do not include that practice realize what a great gift it would be to have absolution (forgiveness) declared to them every Sunday since it is so hard to forgive ourselves. A confession that is most helpful is one which is not so particular that someone could say, "I'm not guilty of that sin," but that is universal so that no one can escape from its truthful application. The word of absolution that is most beneficial is one which clearly and totally announces complete forgiveness through God's Triune mercy. Everyone is a sinner and sins; the practice of joining in corporate confession and hearing words of forgiveness frees us from the burden of our sins and guilt. Here is an example:

> *Pastor [P]:* Most merciful God,
> *Congregation [C]:* we confess that we are in bondage to sin and cannot free ourselves. We have sinned against you in thought, word, and deed, by what we have done and by what we have left undone. We have not loved you with our whole heart; we have not loved our neighbors as ourselves. For the sake of your Son, Jesus Christ, have mercy on us. Forgive us, renew us, and lead us, so

that we may delight in your will and walk in
your ways, to the glory of your holy name.
Amen.
P: In the mercy of almighty God, Jesus Christ
was given to die for you, and for his sake
God forgives you all your sins. To those who
believe in Jesus Christ he gives the power to
become the children of God and bestows on
them the Holy Spirit.
C: Amen.[16]

In the following chart, the general pattern of
the historic Western (as different from the Orthodox) worship service is outlined and elaborated
so that the value of its various parts might be
more clearly seen. Italicized Latin names are often
the first words in the text of particular parts of
the ancient service. Various denominations position the elements of the heritage in diverse ways,
and all sorts of early to modern melodies are used
for those parts which are sung. Both new and old
musical settings often cross denominational lines.

Originally many of the parts—the Scripture
lessons and Psalm for the Day, the "Introit" and
"Collect" and "Gradual" explained below—were
chosen by the larger Church so that worship

would be the same in every place. Today many churches follow what is called the Revised Common Lectionary, which establishes a cycle of readings for three years and utilizes Gospel lessons according to the time of the church year primarily from Matthew, Mark, and Luke in consecutive years. (John is read in special seasons, especially during the Sundays after Easter.) The value of this practice is both that many churches throughout the world read Scripture in common and that much more of the whole Bible is read in the course of three years.

□ □

GENERAL PATTERN OF THE CHURCH'S WORSHIP

Element	Explanation or Example	Why This Element Is Used
□ □ □ □ □ □ **The Gathering** □ □ □ □ □ □		
Invocation	"In the name of the Father and of the Son and of the Holy Spirit. Amen."	Said to remember our baptism in that name and to be reminded for whom our worship is and by whom it is made possible.

Element	Explanation or Example	Why This Element Is Used
Confession and Absolution	(See above.)	—
Introit	An Entrance Hymn or Psalm	Though this might be any hymn, Introits established in earlier centuries set the theme for this particular day of the church year.
Greeting	*P:* "The grace of our Lord Jesus Christ, the love of God, and the communion of the Holy Spirit be with you all." *C:* "And also with you."	This reminds worshippers that they and their leaders are in community together and with the Trinity.
Kyrie ("Lord")	Prayer for the Church and those who worship here	To each phrase the people respond, often in singing, "Lord, have mercy."
Gloria	A Hymn of Praise	This hymn is usually not used in Advent or Lent, which are seasons of penitence.
The Collect	The Prayer of the Day	It gathers the people into the theme of the day's texts and the time in the church year. Many Collects are very old and used

Element	Explanation or Example	Why This Element Is Used
The Collect (continued)		globally. Usually they are proceeded by *P:* "The Lord be with you." *C:* "And also with you."

□ □ □ □ □ □ □ **The Word** □ □ □ □ □ □ □

Element	Explanation or Example	Why This Element Is Used
Old Testament Lesson	Matches the Gospel or sometimes follows a sequence from the same book for several weeks	Often followed by *P:* "The Word of the Lord." *C:* "Thanks be to God!"
Psalm	Matches the theme of the day	Sometimes read antiphonally or chanted.
Epistle Lesson	Matches the Gospel or books read in sequence	Followed by the refrain, *P:* "The Word of the Lord." *C:* "Thanks be to God!"
Gradual	An example is this song from John 6:68: "Alleluia. Lord, to whom shall we go? You have the words of eternal life. Alleluia. Alleluia!"	A song or reading that either matches the day in the church year or is a standard refrain that moves the congregation to the first high point of the service, the Gospel.

How Has the Church Developed Its Ascribing?

Element	Explanation or Example	Why This Element Is Used
Announcement of the Gospel	Announced with the Acclamation: "Glory be to you, O Lord!"	Acclamations are said or sung to accent the Gospel as the high point of worship.
Gospel Lesson	Followed by the Acclamation: "Praise be to you, O Christ!"	——
The Sermon		
The Hymn of the Day	A response to, and application of, the Scriptures and sermon	——
The Apostles' or the Nicene Creed	A confession of the faith that knits the community together	——
The Prayers of the People	Often uses a congregational response after each petition	——
The Passing of the Peace	People say to each other, "May the peace of the Lord be with you."	Makes sure that all members are reconciled before bringing their offering and coming to the Lord's Table.
The Offering	The offering is gathered.	——
Singing of the Offertory	Sometimes "Create in me a clean heart,	

Element	Explanation or Example	Why This Element Is Used
Singing of the Offertory (continued)	O God" from Psalm 51	—
Offering Prayer		

□ □ □ □ □ □   **The Meal**   □ □ □ □ □ □

Element	Explanation or Example	Why This Element Is Used
The Great Thanksgiving	*P:* "The Lord be with you." *C:* "And also with you." *P:* "Lift up your hearts." *C:* "We lift them to the Lord." *P:* "Let us give thanks to the Lord our God." *C:* "It is right to give our thanks and praise."	Unites the pastor and people and points them to the second high point of the service.
The Preface and Eucharistic Prayer	The Preface is appropriate to the season of the church year.	Many ancient versions of this prayer have been recovered; it expresses gratitude for all God's actions in history and especially in Christ.
The *Sanctus*	(See below in section IX.)	—

Element	Explanation or Example	Why This Element Is Used
The Words of Institution	"Our Lord Jesus, the night in which He was betrayed, took bread . . ." from 1 Corinthians 11	—
The Lord's Prayer		
The *Agnus Dei*	"Lamb of God, you take away the sin of the world; have mercy on us. Lamb of God, you take away the sin of the world; have mercy on us. Lamb of God, you take away the sin of the world; grant us your peace."	Reminds us that our salvation was costly to Christ and that we need His mercy profoundly.
Participation in the Meal	Often meditative hymns are sung during the distribution of the meal.	—
The *Nunc Dimittis*	Simeon's song: "Lord, now let your servant depart in peace; your word has been fulfilled . . ." or some other Post-Communion Canticle or Hymn	—

Element	Explanation or Example	Why This Element Is Used
□ □ □ □ □ □ □ **Sending** □ □ □ □ □ □ □		
Closing Prayer	Thanksgiving for the Meal	Expresses confidence in the Meal's blessings.
Benediction	Usually the threefold Aaronic benediction from Numbers 6:24-26	—
Final Hymn	—	—
Commissioning	*P:* "Go in peace. Serve the Lord." *C:* "Thanks be to God!	—

□ □

Of course, there are many advantages and disadvantages to using such a form from the ancient liturgies of the Church's earliest centuries. Among the advantages, as can be readily seen, is that such a liturgy includes many refrains in which young children can participate. Furthermore, the structure requires constant participation by the entire assembly so worshipers have little opportunity to be passive. Also, many of the refrains and sung portions of the liturgy are direct quotations of

Scripture, so the entire service is bathed in the Word. Finally, the service does not depend on the personality of the pastor or worship leader because the interactions are biblical quotations that eliminate private commentary. Rather, the leadership is larger than that of an individual person because the prayers and refrains knit together those who have followed this ancient pattern for centuries and around the globe.

The major disadvantage is that these refrains can become mere rote and lose the power of the Word. Leaders can forget why they are saying these texts and just recite them without life. Also, sometimes the rituals are developed with empty pomp instead of being engaged in with honest gestures. For these reasons, this form of the universal (or catholic) ancient Mass began to be replaced in history with several major trajectories.

The liturgical structure requires constant participation by the entire assembly so worshipers have little opportunity to be passive.

There is not space here to delineate details in the differences between the fundamental branches of the universal Church, but over time particular emphases can be noted and identified more strongly with one group rather than another. Though I am sketching numerous centuries in a few sentences, it seems to me safe to say that until after the major splits between Eastern Orthodoxy and Western Catholicism and then with various principal Reformations, worship was always centered on God and was not usually confused with evangelism. In fact, in the early Church those who were not yet baptized and fully committed to the life and practices of Christian disciples were dismissed from worship and not even permitted to observe when the time came for the Lord's Supper (also called Communion or the Meal or the Eucharist, from the Greek word for "thanksgiving").

Worship had two high points—the Gospel and the Lord's Supper. That Martin Luther in the sixteenth century agreed entirely with this catholic understanding of worship is signalled by his frequent references to true worship as that which contained the Word and Sacraments (including confession/absolution, the Lord's Supper, and baptism).

Several major variations from the primary structure of worship should be noted. The first is the trajectory away from having the Lord's Supper at every Sunday worship service. Of course, early in the history of the Church other forms of worship had been developed, such as the prayer offices of the monastics, but in general churches offered the Holy Meal quite regularly. After the Reformation, more emphasis was put on the Word, and preaching came to

> In the early Church, worship had two high points—the Gospel and the Lord's Supper.

have a much more dominant place so that the twin high points of Gospel and Sacrament were sometimes reduced to one, with greater attention to teaching. Consequently, the structure in many churches developed into a three-fold pattern of Gathering, the Word, and Sending, with the first and last parts concentrating mostly on the singing of songs or hymns or psalms to prepare for the extended sermon. Notice that this variant begins the move away from worship being for God and towards the persuasion that worship was primarily for the instruction of the people.

A second type of major variation which should be noted arose as an antidote to an overly cerebral/doctrinal emphasis on the objective Word. This could be called the Pietist strand of worship. Its major mark was its focus on devotion, adoration, and the language of the "heart," understood in a subjective sense. The great value of this strand is its recovery of emotions which had been and continue to be frequently lost in many forms of biblical instruction. One unstable tendency of this strand, however, is to accentuate only the emotional side and thus lose from the single remaining high point its dialectical interplay of objective truth about God and subjective response of the believer.

The charismatic movement extends this Pietistic trajectory much more extensively and thus gives the greatest freedom in the Spirit for emotional expression. The tendency it must be careful to avoid is the danger of losing the "public" sense of worship since not all participants in a worship service are equally endowed with the same charismatic manifestations. Also, the biblical directive that speaking in tongues should always be "interpreted" in public settings should not be ignored.

A third major variant of the predominant worship structure arose in the mixing of worship and evangelism. John Wesley's public altar calls were given in the fields where he preached and from which he attempted to place converts into churches for worship, but soon "tent meetings" were moved into large tabernacles and then churches. As a result, now many denominations customarily offer evangelistic messages and "altar calls" during the congregation's primary worship time.

All three of these strands are very evident in the range of worship options in contemporary churches in North America. Some churches, most notably those in the Reformed traditions, spend the larger part of the worship service in the Word/sermon, prefacing it with singing and responding to it with more singing. Some churches, particularly those who call their services "Praise and Worship," follow the Pietists' lead. Especially since the 1960s and the Jesus Movement, "Praise and Worship" has specialized in contemporary choruses that emphasize adoration and emotional response to God.

The tent meeting/evangelistic rally trajectory is evident in those churches that sponsor "seeker services." This dimension has been heightened in the last few decades because of stagnation in mainline churches and because of renewed zeal for non-believers in reaction to the complacency of many churches. We discussed the problem of confusing worship and evangelism in section IV above, and we will consider evangelism further in section X below.

What is important for us to recognize now is that each of these trajectories of worship patterns emphasizes something crucial. The Catholic Mass remembers that our Lord Jesus commanded us to eat His Supper when we gather together. The Reformed emphasis on the Word retains the Jewish synagogue pattern of hearing the Scriptures read and having someone teach about that text (see the story of Jesus in his hometown synagogue in Luke 4). The Pietistic trajectory preserves the focus on God and on offering our adoration to Him, while those who offer seeker services remember that keeping the first great commandment to love and worship God must cause believers to keep the second, which is to act in love toward their neighbors and to invite them also to share in the faith.

Consequently, my goal in this book has been to sketch several important questions by means of which congregations can learn—from the Scriptures primarily and other trajectories secondarily—what worship should and could be. Recognizing that many of the aspects over which we fight are simply opposite sides of crucial dialectics which should be held in tension instead of discarding one pole and overemphasizing the other could help us search for ways to keep more of these elements in our worship services. More study of the Scriptures, of

My goal in this book has been to sketch several important questions by means of which congregations can learn what worship should and could be.

worship through the ages, of who God is and how we can best "ascribe to the LORD the glory of His name" would help all our congregations be more faithful in worship.

IX How Will True Worship Change Our Character?

Bring an offering, and come into His courts.
Worship the LORD in holy attire;
  Tremble before Him, all the earth.

PSALM 96:8b-9

In section IV above we noted the structure of the first six lines of Psalm 96 and its literary device of staircase parallelism to create a rousing call to praise ("Sing to the LORD") and then an ardent invitation to evangelism ("Proclaim good tidings. . . . Tell of His glory, . . . His wonderful deeds"). Now that staircase structure is expanded with three more steps into a nine-line stairway in which the original six lines (vv. 1-3) are matched in a three-line call to worship ("Ascribe" in verses 7-8a) and a three-line description of the subject of our evangelistic witness ("Say among the nations" in 9b-10) with an intervening three lines about the way in which we worship ("Bring an offering, and come. . . . Worship . . . in holy attire; Tremble").

This elaborate structure, which might not seem very important, actually fulfills a crucial purpose for our questions in this book, because the intervening three lines, between the matching subjects of worship and evangelism, tell us how we worship and how our character is formed by that worship so that we can be evangelists.

The first command in verse 8b is to bring an offering. Jewish worship involved many different kinds of offering—for sin, as thanksgiving, to make peace, and offerings of praise. If we really think about the truth that worship is for God, then actually all of the worship service is offering.[17] It would help us all to worship more faithfully if we would remember that every element of our participation is our offering, instead of reducing the offering merely to the giving of money at one point in the service. If preachers would give their sermons and musicians their music as

It would help us all to worship more faithfully if we would remember that every element of our participation is our offering.

offerings, then the tendency to perform would be avoided entirely. If those in the pews gave their full attention to sermons and their participation in the liturgy and songs as offerings, then there would be no passivity.

Such a sense of offering in worship, furthermore, would strengthen the habit of character so that all of life could be understood as offering and as worship. How different our daily lives would be if we perceived them not as an endless round of chores to accomplish, but as a continuing variety of opportunities to bring an offering to the LORD!

The question might then be raised, if all of life is worship, then why come to a church building or worship center for "public, corporate" worship? Psalm 96:8b suggests an answer with the phrase, "come into His courts." The Hebrew word which we translate "courts" probably refers to the open area where the Israelites stood in the Temple precincts, which they perceived as a place where the LORD's presence could be especially experienced. Furthermore, the verb *come* is plural. Perhaps we should translate the phrase, "y'all come into the LORD's presence" or, as a

> **H**ow different our daily lives would be if we perceived them not as an endless round of chores to accomplish, but as a continuing variety of opportunities to bring an offering to the LORD!

117

Georgian gentleman informed me, with the true Southern plural, "all y'all come. . . ."

It is not enough to worship alone. God is too great to be comprehended by my little mind or to be adequately honored with my feeble praises. I need to hear other voices, learn from preachers, benefit from the gifts of an entire community, be part of a great company of singers, pray with all the saints. Even more glorious, various passages in the Scriptures, especially in the book of Revelation, invite us to envision ourselves as part of the entire host of God's people who worship Him eternally.

Do your worship services give participants the sense that your congregation does not worship alone, that the great saints of all times are present with you? What can we do in our corporate praise to have a greater awareness that the whole people of God worship here? Some older churches, for example, foster that consciousness with their architecture; when the worshipers gather around the altar for the Lord's Supper, they kneel at a rail shaped as a half circle and perceive that the other half of the circle is in heaven.

The ancient catholic liturgy includes at the beginning of the Sunday order for the Lord's Supper a "Preface" appropriate to the season of the church year, which concludes with this line spoken by the pastor or priest: "Therefore we praise you, joining our voices with Angels and Archangels and with all the company of heaven, who forever sing this hymn to proclaim the glory of your Name"—and then the entire congregation sings the *Sanctus,* the ancient Jewish and Christian hymn of adoration: "Holy, holy, holy, LORD God of power and might! Heaven and earth are full of your glory. Hosanna in the highest. Blessed is He who comes in the name of the LORD. Hosanna in the highest."[18]

Because of its cosmic connections, I love singing this ancient hymn (which has been set to many glorious melodies old and new). The first lines of the text come from Isaiah 6, where seraphim sing it antiphonally. The second half of the text (which quotes Psalm 118:26) was shouted by the children on Palm Sunday, so whenever we sing it we join the children at Jerusalem and all the saints throughout time and space to welcome Jesus into our lives. When I was teaching in Madagascar and Poland, I joined with saints in those places to sing it. Many denominations around the globe sing it. Altogether, that is a colossal cosmic choir! When we sing the *Sanctus* on Sunday mornings and are conscious that people have chanted this hymn since at least seven hundred years before Christ, we experience an immersion into the great "cloud of witnesses" (see Hebrews 11:1–12:1) that cheer on our faith!

To comprehend that we worship with all the saints throughout time and space will likewise influence our character for daily life, for we begin to realize that we do our work and witness also surrounded by this cloud of saints. I'm convinced that it makes it easier for our children to go to their schools where they might be teased for their faith if they know that they go there in the company of the saints and the hosts of heaven. All of us can be more bold to proclaim the good news of God's grace in Christ if we remember that we testify as part of a great crowd of believers.

When we all together "come into [God's] courts," we learn the language of faith from the whole people of God. To learn this language is essential for daily life because Christianity is no longer the dominant culture of our society. If we want to *live* as Christians, we need to learn the faith's language about time, money, possessions, love, sex, marriage, family, work, power, our relationship with our neighbors, and so forth. Sociologists recognize that any group (Christian or otherwise) that advocates an alternative way of life significantly different from the larger society needs such a language, a worldview, a coherent way of thinking about things. Gathering with others for worship and sharing in its rituals teaches us practices and habits of prayer and praise, offering and testimony. This is a language that tells us who we are, reminds us of our identity in relationship with God and neighbors, upholds and nurtures our vision of how we are different and why that matters.

> **T**o learn this language [of faith] is essential for daily life because Christianity is no longer the dominant culture of our society.

In our culture, the predominant way of thinking is usually defined by technology and consumerism; we comprehend life in terms of various devices that produce commodities. Every aspect of society is endangered by this paradigm—that education should produce grades and high scores on tests instead of supporting students' engagement in the processes of learning; that doctors and nurses dispense medicines and techniques that produce health, instead of engaging with their patients in practices that promote total well-being. Even churches fall prey to this device/commodity paradigm when we let worship styles be the device to produce "attraction" and large numbers, instead of forming believers who offer their lives in deep engagement with their neighbors—in hospitality, compassion, witness.

Holy Attire or the Splendor of Holiness

The first line of Psalm 96:9 has been variously translated by English versions and thereby can cause some confusion. Is the text commanding that we "worship the LORD in holy attire" so that it is imperative that we "dress up" when we participate in public worship on Sunday mornings? Or does the text mean that we worship in "holy splendor" (NRSV), "in all his holy splendor" (NLT), or "in the splendor of his holiness" (NIV)? It seems to make a big difference if the psalm is talking about our attire or holiness and, if the latter, whether the holiness is ours or God's.

The Hebrew word translated "attire" or "splendor" is actually another form of the second noun in verse 6, which the New American Standard Bible translates as "majesty," so the term definitely means more than simply what we wear.

Furthermore, the noun is in a construct form that links it directly to the noun for "holiness." It is a splendor, majesty, beauty inextricably connected with holiness.

Immediately I think that I can't worship God in such a way. I certainly have no holiness of my own with which to praise Him. Only through the salvific work of Christ, who then clothes me with His righteousness (see Philippians 3:8-9 and Ephesians 6:13-14), can we come into God's presence to worship. Thus, in answer to our questions above, the psalm is talking about both our attire and holiness, and the holiness is both God's and ours. We worship attired in God's holiness, and that forms our character to be like His.

In fact, the more we worship the LORD and ascribe to Him the glory, honor, and strength of His Name, the more our character will be formed

> **W**e worship attired in God's holiness, and that forms our character to be like His.

in His likeness. Paul tells the Corinthians, "But we all, with unveiled face beholding as in a mirror the glory of the Lord, are being transformed into the same image from glory to glory, just as from the Lord, the Spirit" (2 Corinthians 3:18).

There still remains the minor question—which causes fights in some churches—of what our physical attire should be for worship. Once again, two dialectical poles are set in opposition to each other instead of held in tension. On the one side is the desire to "dress up" to honor the "King of kings, and LORD of lords" (Revelation 19:16). When on a college concert tour around the world we sang a command performance for the king of Thailand, we made sure our concert uniforms were in their best shape and took extra care with our hair. Wouldn't we do much more for the King of the universe?

One of the most glorious sights in my memory occurred in a worship service in Madagascar when hundreds of teenagers and young children, all dressed in white—which made their beautiful ebony skin even more stunning—made a procession to the altar to deliver their monetary offerings. They had already given many offerings of magnificent singing and their avid participation in the liturgy. In that culture, they all wore their best for worship (even as they sang their best).

Those who argue for dressing our best make two important truthful points: that God deserves our special offering of taking time to come attired in our best and that dressing our best often influences our behavior and teaches us to act with more civility and graciousness. The first point was stronger in past societies in which people might have only two changes of clothes—one for work and one for "Sunday best." The second argument actually has social evidence in improved behavior when schools require children to follow a dress code.

On the other side, many in North America believe that folks won't come to worship if they have to dress up. The point is often emphasized that "God takes you just as you are." This side of the argument also holds other very important truths, such as these: in many churches holy days become fashion shows, with women subtly competing for everyone's adoration of their elaborate outfits; in some churches poor people who don't have special clothes feel too much out of place to come; in our culture many no longer dress specially for work, so casual dressing is the common habit for all things. At concerts of the Oregon Symphony, for example, audience attire ranges from black evening clothes to blue jeans.

This might seem like a petty subject to waste this space, but I have introduced it because it offers a good example of how better questions could help us think through issues on which people disagree in order to find better responses. Some of the questions I ask myself about dressing are these: has either side become an idolatry—of being comfortable or of refinement? If Jesus were to walk into the sanctuary where we are worshiping, what would I want to have on my mind and on my body? How do I dress for company? How do I prepare for being with people I love? Most important, how am I preparing my body, my mind, and my heart before I come to worship for what will happen there?

Some of the questions our congregations could ask are these: does a poorly dressed person feel welcome in our congregation? Does the affluence of our congregation express itself in an idolatry of clothes? Does the idolatry of personal comfort invade our worship? How will we better learn as a people to clothe ourselves with the LORD's holiness? How can our worship services more fully display the LORD's glory, so that, beholding it, members of the congregation become transformed into His image? How will our demeanor and dress for worship influence our formation in Christian character?

In all of our questioning, the ultimate goal is that as we gather to praise the LORD in our worship services one result will be that we are formed to be people whose character displays our relationship with God. Will the practice of offering our voices, hearts, lives, and resources to the LORD in worship form us then to offer all of our daily lives to God in praise? Will the realization that we are able to worship because we are clothed in Christ's holiness free us to live each day in the same sense of grace? Now as we turn to the last dimension of these lines in Psalm 96 concerning the ways in which we worship, let us consider how we tremble and how it would affect our character to perceive always that only through God's immense mercy are we able to worship Him. How would it affect our daily lives if we never took worship for granted?

The Great Privilege of Worship

The second line of Psalm 96:9 has caused interpreters some differences—as evidenced by the rendering in the New Revised Standard Version of the Bible as "tremble before him" and in the New English Bible as "dance in his honor." Is this a command of fear or of festivity? How does the command for all the earth to tremble before the LORD affect our worship and, consequently, the development of our character as believers?

We can find some help with these questions by comparing Psalm 96 with the earlier Psalm 29, from which some lines were borrowed. Psalm 29 begins with three commands to "Ascribe to the LORD" that are similar to, but not identical with, those in Psalm 96:7-8a. Then the same verb, which our version above translates "tremble," is used twice in Psalm 29:8 and rendered "shakes" in this context:

The voice of the LORD is upon the waters;
   The God of glory thunders,
   The LORD is over many waters.
The voice of the LORD is powerful,
   The voice of the LORD is majestic. . . .
The voice of the LORD shakes the wilderness,
   The LORD shakes the wilderness of Kadesh.
   (Psalm 29:3-4, 8)

It is obvious that the poem is considering God's power in nature, as well as in history, for the wilderness of Kadesh was a symbol of Israel's disobedience (see Numbers 32:8, Deuteronomy 1:46;

9:23; 32:51). Deuteronomy 32:51 is especially important because the LORD reminds Moses, "You broke faith with Me, . . . you did not treat Me as holy," and therefore, though Moses is enabled to see the Promised Land, God denies him the possibility of entering it. We tremble in God's presence because our sinfulness has consequences.

It seems to me that the command in Psalm 96, correlatively, reminds us that we have no right to worship the LORD. We can do so only because of God's immense forgiveness and condescension. An awareness of this will fill us with profound wonder at the great privilege of worship and the enormous gift of God's pardon! Two dimensions of this consciousness require further discussion.

The first dimension relates to the contemporary trend not to talk about sin in worship. Some marketing gurus insist that the word *sin* should not be used because it makes visitors to worship uncomfortable or because it lowers people's self-esteem. Actually, biblical texts (and commonplace experiences, too) have convinced me of the opposite: people in our culture *want* to talk about sin (though they might not know it) because they are starved for genuine forgiveness. Furthermore, since we all know deep down that we can't do what we want to do and often don't do what we wish (see Romans 7), our self-esteem cannot be boosted by false—and therefore trivial—assurances that we are okay. Instead, we will find the highest self-esteem in the gift and then practical acknowledgement that we are forgiven by the Triune God who calls us "beloved."

Thus, we tremble at worship because we come as sinners. However, when we begin the worship service with a confession of sin and the pastor or priest pronounces a clear word of forgiveness in Christ's name, this powerful ritual frees us to enjoy God's presence and it forms us to live as forgiven people instead of walking around daily life with a load of guilt. The pastoral proclamation of absolute reconciliation with God, entirely by means of God's pardoning mercy, is one of the greatest gifts of the worship service because it is usually not possible for us to forgive ourselves. The explicit announcement that *all* my sins, known and unknown, have been pardoned through Jesus Christ is the best good news available anywhere in the world. Why on earth would our churches not want to speak these glad tidings to guilty and burdened hearts? And won't it change our lives immensely if worship frees us to live as forgiven saints, instead of encumbered sinners, loaded with regrets and faults? Furthermore, the act of confession and absolution in a worship service also trains us to practice repentance and forgiveness in our daily lives, for Jesus

The pastoral proclamation of absolute reconciliation with God, entirely by means of God's pardoning mercy, is one of the greatest gifts of the worship service.

gave the power to forgive sins to all of us who are members of His Body, the Church.

The second topic raised by Psalm 96's command to "tremble" involves the fundamental reason which motivates our attendance at worship services. Earlier in this book we considered the problem when people choose what kind of worship service they want to attend, especially when one congregation offers various styles of worship and members become consumers of the kind they like. Here we should look at an even thornier problem—the subversion of genuine worship that happens when we turn attending worship into a matter of our own choice instead of obedience to God's command and the reception of sheer grace.

We live in a society of choices, often to our own befuddlement. We have innumerable

choices of breakfast food, countless possibilities
for entertainment, more options than we can in-
telligently manage for purchasing technological
gadgets and tools, more alternatives for spending
our time than we have time to decide. Too many
choices is one of many reasons that Christianity is
declining in North America—there are far too
many supposedly better things to do on Sunday
mornings and far too many other possibilities for
making sense of our lives.

One of the worst things that has happened to
the faith formation of our churches' children is
that parents follow our society's principles in let-
ting their offspring choose whether to participate
in public worship. I am forever grateful to my
parents (and God) that in our family not worshiping was never a choice. My earliest training was
from my mother, who always pointed to the
words in the hymnal long before I could read, so
that I became eager to learn to participate and was
enabled to be involved to the limits of my infant
capacities. I wish *every* mother helped her children follow along and be engaged as mine did.[19]

Whenever the people of God gathered for corporate worship, we were there—every Sunday,
every Wednesday evening in Lent, for all the

special services of Holy Week and for several services on Easter and Christmas. I am so thankful that my parents thereby instilled in me the delightful and formative habit of weekly worship early in my childhood. Now I joke that this habit saves a lot of time—because my husband and I never waste time on Sunday mornings deciding whether to participate in worship. We simply go. (It is similar to the habit of tithing. We never have to ask *if* we will tithe. It is simply what both my husband and I learned as children that God's people do! In fact, the question for all of us in North America—who are so rich compared with the rest of the globe—could perhaps be what percentage beyond 10 percent we can give for God's purposes. Could we make it half of all we make?)

The habit of regular worship is especially glorious because it formed me to tremble before the LORD and never take for granted the privilege of worship, to want always to keep God central in my life, and to undertake my existence according to a spiritual calendar and not by the world's. My week be-

> **T**he habit of regular worship is especially glorious because it formed me to tremble before the LORD and never take for granted the privilege of worship.

gins with the Joy of worship and of Sabbath keeping,[20] which empower me for the work of the week to come. In addition, the habit of worship has taught me to reckon the year's seasons not by the weather, but by rhythms of repentance (we could say, the trembling) and longing and preparation (in Advent, Lent, and Ascension), celebration (at Christmas, Easter, and Pentecost), and proclamation of the mighty acts of God (during Epiphany, the forty days after Easter, and the Pentecost season). To that proclamation we now turn.

X How Does the LORD's Sovereignty Affect Our Worship and Evangelism?

Say among the nations, "The LORD reigns;
  Indeed, the world is firmly established, it will
    not be moved;
  He will judge the peoples with equity."

PSALM 96:10

Psalm 96:10 reports the message of our evangelism, telling us what to "say among the nations" and thereby helping us to know more deeply what we learn when we gather to praise God. In the previous section, we considered how worshiping God forms our character: nurturing us to understand all of life as worship and offering, equipping us with a sense of the LORD's holiness at work through us, delighting us with the freedom of forgiveness and the obligation/privilege of responding with praise. One other aspect of worship emphasized by this psalm is that when we "sing to the LORD" and "ascribe to the LORD the glory of His name," we will become so aware of God's magnificence that we will want to tell our neighbors—and all the nations.

When "the Lᴏʀᴅ reigns" in our lives, then we will want to help others know the Joy of His reign. When we see the fullness of God's sovereignty in establishing the world so firmly, we will want our neighbors to know that trust and confidence are possible in the midst of global political and economic insecurities. In a grossly unjust world in which the rich are favored, we will eagerly proclaim God's ultimate justice and impartiality.

All of these declarations are strong. The message of Christianity is indeed good news in an unbalanced world. The Trinity gives firm foundations to life; all is not unmoored, tottering, chaotic, collapsing. In our increasingly postmodern times, many people are looking for moral underpinnings, some basis for security, some promise of safety, some hope for a radiant future.

What worship does is redescribe the world! If we look at things from a human perspective,

What worship does is redescribe the world!

there is massive evidence and cause for fear, anxiety, doubt, even despair. But in worship we see God truly and learn the LORD's sovereignty over our own lives and over the life of the cosmos. We learn to look for signs that "heaven and earth are full of [God's] glory," as Isaiah 6 and the *Sanctus* declare. We recount the biblical narratives that show God's Lordship over the nations and Christ's triumph over the powers of evil.

How do we get a big enough picture to redescribe the world? One element in the fights over worship that confuses me is that sometimes churches who are most adamant about being biblically based use less of Scripture in worship services. Whereas churches that share the Revised Common Lectionary customarily incorporate three or four lessons from the Bible in each worship service—an Old Testament lesson, a Psalm (perhaps chanted), an Epistle reading, and a Gospel text—churches from "free church" traditions might employ only one passage or even just a few verses.

Once again, we recognize two dialectical truths. We need to hear more of the Scriptures to gain a better sense of the whole biblical meta-narrative, the master account of God's attributes and actions for the sake of the world from its beginning to the culmination of God's kingdom at the end of time. On the other side, we need to look deeply into texts to mine more thoroughly their treasures.

As with all other dialectical combinations in this book, this one requires that we ask better questions about our churches' use of the Scriptures in worship. Do we, over the course of time, expose worship participants to "the whole counsel of God"? Does each worship service give them a sense of the vast meta-narrative, of the larger framework in which the particular texts of the day are embedded? Do our sermons redescribe the world and paint a full picture of the kingdom of God so that the listeners can enter into it and live its truths throughout the week? Do our worship services fill participants with such Joy in God's sovereignty that they eagerly tell their neighbors about God's reign? In other words, is the picture of God in worship so comprehensive that the saints are equipped to live the rest of the week as missional people?

One other dimension of God's sovereignty should be considered, and this relates to present-day fights over how much we can use cultural elements in worship. For example, one pastor whose worship strategies are widely copied advocates using secular songs, a pastoral presence resembling that of a talk-show host, building sanctuaries that offer worship participants coffee-cup holders at their auditorium-style seats, and removing Christian symbolism from the worship place. Should our worship places be distinctly Christian? Should worship employ distinctly Christian songs? Should the pastor wear robes or in some other way evidence a sense of biblical authority? Should non-Christian readings, such as Native American prayers, be used?

All of these questions cannot be rightly considered unless we keep in mind the fundamental questions raised in sections II and IX of this book: *Who* is being worshiped? and How will true worship *change our charac-ter*? These questions can be elaborated with queries such as these: How can we continually give worshipers

Fundamental questions: *Who* is being worshiped? and How will true worship *change our character*?

the sense that they have entered God's presence and that they don't deserve to be there, but are instead welcomed by grace? How can we help believers know that the authority of the Scriptures is different from that of any other book in the world? How can we more deeply help the saints become the people of God so that they live differently from non-Christians in daily life? How can we make sure that those who learn with different senses are also deepened in their awareness of the fullness of God's presence?

I ask the last question because it seems to me that the presence of Christian symbols deepens our worship, for we can feast our eyes on large Bibles (to keep reminding us that the Word is bigger than we are!), banners, altar cloths, icons, carvings, sculptures, crosses, candles, lamps representing the constant light of the Holy Spirit, paintings, stained-glass windows, flowers, liturgical colors, nativity scenes, chalices of wine/grape juice and plates of bread for the Lord's Supper, baptismal fonts, or other visual aids to teach us more about who God is and how God is present. There is a great gift in setting this worship space aside as a holy place, where its entire ambience—fragrances, textures, tastes, sights, and sounds—reminds us that what we do here is not like what we do anywhere else because here our complete attention is fixed on God.

Many argue that such a "holy" place alienates

strangers and seekers—and that might be true. However, we must keep remembering that evangelism is not the primary purpose of the worship service, but rather the work of all the church members in their daily lives, and its outcome is that we bring our neighbors to worship. If we are hospitable, if we explain the meanings of the symbols to those for whom they are not familiar, if we do all that we can to introduce our friends to what worship is and why it matters, then they will feel at home in our friendship until they discover the deeper home of God's presence.

The critical difference between Christians and non-Christians is whether we genuinely worship the true God. For that reason, all our questions about using secular elements for worship require careful consideration of how much cultural forms can be used without losing the biblical character of churches and their worship.

Of course, we can't escape cultural forms. We use our native language, various styles of singing from cultural eras, instruments and books that were developed by past and present cultures. There is always, for all our churches, the need for a delicate balancing of using the gifts of our culture without having the faith conditioned falsely

by them. Too much alignment with non-Christian
influences prevents us from truly forming *Christians*. Too much alienation from the surrounding
culture prevents us from learning how to speak
the language of faith in our times and places.[21]
Each congregation must constantly ask about
their worship, *Who* is being worshiped? and How
will true worship *change our character*?

If we are truly formed to be wholly God's people, then our witness to the world will be more
believable. The world needs to see a way of life
that gives warrant for belief. If our lives demonstrate our participation in God's kingdom, then
the nations will comprehend it and desire it when
we say to them, "The LORD reigns."

XI | How Does the Creation Teach Us to Praise?

Let the heavens be glad, and let the earth rejoice;
  Let the sea roar, and all it contains;
Let the field exult, and all that is in it.
  Then all the trees of the forest will sing for joy
Before the LORD, for He is coming;

PSALM 96:11-13a

The lines from Abraham Joshua Heschel at the beginning of this book pointed to creation as a model for our praise. Psalm 96:11-13a shows us that elements of nature teach us one of the most important lessons about worship's subject. All the facets of creation live their whole being in praise: the heavens, the earth, the sea and all its creatures, the field and all its inhabitants, the trees all give glory to the LORD. And why? They rejoice because He is coming!

The Hebrew verbs in this whole set of lines are continuing verbs translated as exhortations, so it is a perpetual gladness and rejoicing and singing that the creation exhibits. All the verbs are re-

lated to exuberance, exhilaration, exultation—
except the verb *roar,* in connection with the sea.
That verb picks up the Hebrew root translated
thunder in reference to the "voice of the LORD"—
the phrase repeated seven times in Psalm 29,
which was the source for Psalm 96's later expan-

All the facets of creation live their whole being in praise: all give glory to the LORD. They rejoice because He is coming!

sion. I mention all these details because both
Psalms 29 and 96, in the combination of the verbs
and the images they present of the creation, show
how in the LORD's Temple of the cosmos "everything says, 'Glory!'" (Psalm 29:9c). Psalm 96
especially displays the faithfulness of heavens
and earth, seas and fields, trees and creatures in
freely being what they were created to be before
the LORD now, in anticipation of His culmination
of His reign.

These reflections are important for our considerations of how we worship because our corporate gatherings to praise God immerse us in the
experience of the LORD's coming. Furthermore,
the spaces and places of the cosmos and all their
inhabitants—all God's creations—demonstrate
how to praise, for they do it fully, continuously,

and corporately according to their created being and always in anticipation of their perfection when the LORD comes.

Can we be such creatures, too? Even more important, can we learn to be such creatures together as a community?

One of my greatest concerns for churches in the twenty-first century arises because our culture is so individualized, and worship in many places increasingly seems to be so. The picture in Psalm 96:11-12 shows all of nature joining together in exaltation and exultation (that is, praise to God and corporate rejoicing). Without the marring caused by human sin, the creation was designed in harmony and mutuality and unity to reveal the glory of God. But our churches do not seem to live in such a way.[22]

I have stressed throughout this book that worship is for God and that its major result will be that our character is formed to be like God's. Let me also emphasize here that genuine worship forms us to be a *community* like God in God's triunity.

That is why it is so essential that we deal with conflicts over worship not by splitting into two groups nor by tyrannical (hierarchical or "democratic") decisions that squelch part of the Body (and therefore some of the gifts of the Spirit!). The Church is not a hierarchy, for Jesus Christ is its Head, and we are all equally members of the Body—and "to each one is given the manifestation of the Spirit for the common good" (1 Corinthians 12:7). The Church is not a democracy either, for we don't decide matters of doctrinal truth (or worship issues) by majority vote. Rather, such issues should be decided through communal discussion nurtured by special spiritual gifts.

Instead, what many churches do is decide how to worship on the basis of a survey asking members what they *want* for worship or on the basis of sociological research that reports what society wants. It seems to me that if worship is for God and forms who we are as God's people, then the last thing we should consider in deciding about worship is what people want! What they want might not be good for them or the Body as a whole. Indeed, our churches are concerned to *form Christians and a Christian community,* not cater to consumerist choices.

Worship is certainly countercultural, for it is the opposite of society's idolatries. Furthermore,

it forms believers and the Christian community—
if it is truly biblical—to be unquestionably an alternative society. Decisions about worship, consequently, are reached also in an alternative way.

The faithful Church has never been—and
should never be—a democracy nor a hierarchy.
Rather, it is a *Spiritocracy,* a Body governed by
the Spirit's empowering with Christ as the Head,
and a *charismacracy,* a word I coined to signify
leadership by means of Spirit-endowed gifts (*cha-
risma* in Greek).

If our churches are truly charismacracies, we
will not be controlled by any hierarchies or ma-
jorities of wealth or power, personal tastes or desires, but we will function under the genuine
authority of Spirit-given gifts. Thereby we will
together order our priorities for worship, discern
the time in the church year and the themes of
texts, weigh various options for worship, and
discern which elements will best help us focus on
God and be formed as believers and as a community according to God's patterns illuminated in
the Scriptures (as interpreted by the whole
Church).

The charismacracy which plans worship includes the gifts of the pastor, whose spiritual life

is regularly nourished by personal devotional disciplines, who diligently studies and follows God's Revelation in the Bible, and who listens most of all to God Himself. The pastor explores the meaning of worship and its practice throughout the Church and guides the parish's musicians and worship committee theologically and biblically to design the best, most integrated and congruent way to immerse the worshipers in the "glory and strength" of the LORD revealed in the texts for the day.

The charismacracy also depends upon the gifts of the church's musicians (whether organists or guitarists, flute or violin players, singers or choir directors, whatever). Those who have studied the development of church music throughout the ages can contribute more fully out of that historical awareness, but for all musicians who lead worship it is essential that they practice diligently to hone their skills and study both privately and with the pastor to understand the biblical foundations for each worship service. Also, various denominations and music publishers offer training seminars and reviews of new resources so that musicians can find the best music to immerse worshipers in the "glory and strength" of the LORD as it is revealed in psalms and hymns and songs, melodies and texts, choral anthems and instrumental pieces.

For the purpose of genuinely communal worship, the charismacracy usually also involves a worship committee including a diversity of congregation members (representing different ages, races, social classes, levels of expertise, and spiritual gifts). For the sake of faithfulness, these members would be spiritually diligent, participate regularly in Bible study and worship, learn from worship conferences and other educational options, cooperate together as a team with the pastors and musicians, and glean observations and recommendations from other congregation members so that they could craft worship services that immerse the worshipers in the "glory and strength" of the LORD through every element that the service contains.

These components of theology, musicianship, and committed committee members make it possible for the entire gifted community, under the Holy Spirit's directions, to bring their offerings to the Body's worship. Remember that these are the goals of the charismacracy's offerings: that the focus of the worship service itself will be kept on God, that the members of the entire congregation will be knit into a genuine community, and that the believers will continue to be formed as faithful followers of Christ.

Of course, these are the ideals—and we still live in a sinful world. Our praises will not be perfect until the LORD comes. Our communities will have disagreements over tastes and forms, intentions and purposes. But if we always remember the true purposes of worship, base our decisions on biblical foundations, stay alert to idolatries that easily sneak in, and seek to be a genuine charismacracy through the Holy Spirit's empowerment, then we will keep working to bridge the differences and resolve the conflicts as a *Christian community* (with heavy accent on each of those italicized words). Can we join the heavens and the earth, the sea and land, the plants and creatures, and all the saints throughout time and space as church communities that exalt the LORD with all our best gifts and exult together with all the Joy of the future fulfillment of the Kingdom of God?

XII How Does Worship Form Us by the Future to Live in the Present?

Then all the trees of the forest will sing for joy
Before the LORD, for He is coming;
  For He is coming to judge the earth.
He will judge the world in righteousness,
  And the peoples in His faithfulness.

PSALM 96:12b-13

As we have seen in Psalm 96:11-12, all creation gives us a model for worship—especially because all the cosmos sings "before the LORD, for He is coming." Biblical scholars note that because the phrase *He is coming* is doubled, it underscores the dependability of the LORD's advents. The heavens and the earth and all that is in them proclaim, "Surely He is coming." That is why worship can strongly announce the future of God's kingdom, and why we can base our present lives on it.

Moreover, the LORD comes "to judge the

earth." This verb *to judge* is different from the one in verse 10a and carries connotations not so much of assessing or deciding (with fairness), but more of governing or ruling (in righteousness and faithfulness). The praise of the cosmos declares that, contrary to this world of gross injustice and deluges of deception, God's reign will be marked by justice and truth. (The Hebrew root of the last word of the psalm is the one from which we get our affirmation, *Amen!*)

Consequently, we should always ask of our worship whether it forms us to be people of God's kingdom. When we leave the worship service, has our character been nurtured by visions of God's reign so that we will be agents of Triune righteousness and faithfulness in the world— God's purposes to feed the hungry, combat oppressions, expose the lies, live the truth?

Last evening at midweek Lenten vespers, the pastor spoke on Philippians 3 and asked all of us who were there whether our lives in the present were determined by the past (3:13), the present (3:19), or the future (3:12, 13b-14, 20-21). His question made me realize how crucial this section is for this book.

Many people in our culture find their lives

pulled down by their past. Sometimes the past causes us to live out of guilt or regret. Perhaps the addictions or abuses of our childhood homes seem insurmountable; we might fear the same tendencies in ourselves.

Many other people in our culture live primarily for and out of the present. They crave instant gratification and often are heedless of consequences. Perhaps we, too, let the idols of the moment cause us to live focused only on the immediate.

As believers, we have another option—worship trains us for it!—and that is to live in the present because of, guided by, and with the undergirding of the future. In this section we will consider the interrelationship of worship and living *eschatologically,* which means to live in the light of the *eschaton* (the "end time" or "last times"). How does the future kingdom of God (in many advents) break into the present? How does worship help us let that great future affect our present way of life? How does worship enable us consciously and deliberately to orient our individual lives and corporate life by the future?

I must first stress that I do not mean that worship is only about heaven, nor that our Christian character should be formed to be "so heavenly minded we're no earthly good." Nor do I accept the reductionism of heaven that makes it simply a personal "pie in the sky in the bye and bye when we die."[23] The fact is that eternal life *is* the believers' present possession—notice how the Gospel of John (e.g., John 3:16, 36) always uses present tense verbs in declarations that if you believe, you *have* eternal life. However, though the kingdom has already begun in the incarnated ministry of Jesus (see Mark 1:15), it is not yet completely consummated, so God's people still continue to live in this eschatological tension of "already, but not yet."

To our great loss, this eschatological way of life is not usually remembered—partly because our culture resists any sense of transcendence—but the church's worship could change that, even as cognizance of eschatology will change how we worship! Therefore, in this final section we will consider three aspects of the interrelationship of life and worship:

> **T**he fact is that eternal life *is* the believers' present possession. . . . [But] it is not yet completely consummated, so God's people still continue to live in this eschatological tension of "already, but not yet."

why an eschatological orientation is necessary for both; how worship could be made more eschatological; and how eschatological worship will form us, personally and corporately, for the sake of the world.

Why an Eschatological Orientation Is Necessary for Worship and Life

When the eschatological dimension of our faith is missing, we lose an awe-full lot of the true God! We don't understand thoroughly the utter sufficiency of His grace, or the ultimate triumph of His power. Sermons become therapy instead of proclamation. Worship can become instructions for self-help instead of praiseful recognition that God has already accomplished all that is necessary for our life and salvation. Similarly, unless we keep in mind the truth that God's ultimate reign has already broken into this epoch, when we consider (e.g., in sermons) how to deal with the injustices of the world, we begin to think that to create justice in our world is our work, and not God's through us.

An eschatological orientation is especially important in our worship services and daily life because otherwise we don't deal well with human suffering. Sometimes because churches know that in the future all sorrow and suffering will be gone forever, they suppress or ignore our present pains and the world's current troubles by only singing "happy songs." Contrarily, true eschatology will enable us rather to engage in honest, earnest lament. The book of Psalms is filled with poems that hold in tension both sides—confidence in God's reign and yet genuine expression of grief and confusion. Knowing that the LORD will ultimately triumph and experiencing the beginnings of His reign now frees us to face and admit (as the psalmists do) our sorrows and fears. Jesus who reigns lived among us in the same brokenness—and "for the joy set before Him endured the cross, despising the shame, and has sat down at the right hand of the throne of God" (Hebrews 12:2). Remembering this dialectical combination enables us to be more faithful to the crucified *and* risen Lord, to the Scriptures that continually reveal both sides of the "already but not yet" of eschatology, to the way of life of the Christian community, to the broken realities of our sin-sick world, and to the certainty of God's ultimate triumph over sorrow, sin, death, and the devil at the end of time.[24]

In addition, many of the problems in worship

conflicts could be avoided if we think about worship more eschatologically. For example, it is impossible to turn worship into entertainment if we remember that we are celebrating the reign of the LORD of the cosmos and if our celebration forms us to be people of that reign and thereby plunged into the world's problems as agents of God's purposes. Furthermore, if it is God's reign we are acclaiming, then there is no place for "star clergy" or a "cult of personality." Preachers and musicians will remember that it is not their personalities or manipulative chatter which display God, but their transparency so that the Light of Christ can radiantly shine and the Word of God can be clearly heard through their offerings.

Moreover, since worship affects how persons understand themselves as Christians and what it means to be the corporate Body of the Church, to think eschatologically will guide our choices of songs and hymns for formation. As one example, trivial worship songs will create in people's mind a trivial God and a trivial faith. Because the results of worship styles on the development of a believer's character and the character of the congregational community are enormous, worship planners will take greater care that elements chosen for particular worship services will fit the people for the kingdom of God.

Furthermore, if our worship is more eschatological, then we won't allow any distinctions between people by age or musical taste. Think about this question: "Is heavenly worship for everyone?" Won't "boomers" and "X-ers" all be together some day? Wouldn't it be good preparation for our future life united in glory if we could learn to sing together now across generational lines? Also, our singing together will encourage greater living together—friendships of old and young, service and outreach projects undertaken by multigenerational groups, a genuine restoration of the Christian community as a true *family*.

Finally, an eschatological orientation is crucial so that we don't let worship become utilitarian. When we know that worship praises the LORD for *He* is coming, we will more likely remember that it is not intended to accomplish anything. Perhaps then we can learn more simply to stand in God's presence and to bask in the immensity of God's reign over all of life and the future. Since we know that our future is already made possible by God's grace, we will never forget that our worship on earth will always be inadequate and won't earn us any merit with God.

Knowing that our worship is inadequate won't cause us to give up worshiping or to think that "anything goes" in worship. Rather, it will kindle in us an eagerness to respond to God's lavish grace with the greatest excellence we can develop. We will want to praise our stupendously gracious LORD with the very best we can offer.

How Worship Can Be Made More Eschatological

Worship helps us remember that in spite of all evidence to the contrary, the LORD rules the cosmos. We saw above in section XI that the creation around us (when and where it is unspoiled by our technological manipulations) gives us a model of witness to the LORD's reigning. In planning our public, corporate worship, let us consider how "psalms, hymns, and spiritual songs"; texts, homilies, and sermons; prayers, creeds, and liturgies; Baptism and the Lord's Supper can more constantly remind us of God's kingdom and our future life in His perfect faithfulness.

The ancient Church's prayers seemed to be more eschatologically oriented than prayers today seem to be. For example, the historic prayers shared still by many denominations frequently end with these phrases, "through your only Son, Jesus Christ our Lord, who lives and reigns with you and the Holy Spirit, one God, now and forever." These phrases or others like them could be added to contemporary prayers as a good reminder that Christ governs (because of His triumph over all the evil powers in His life, death, resurrection, ascension) and that the "now"ness of God's reign changes everything, including our understanding of what we have just prayed.

When we make our petitions, how would it affect the way we ask for things if we more clearly kept in mind God's great future and present advents? Wouldn't all our concerns find their bearings more truly if we thought about them with an eternal perspective? For example, if we pray about the hungry of the world, doesn't it encourage us to get busy doing something about their poverty when we publicly remember that God's rule has provided the sun and the rain and the growth of plants already and we are merely the distributors of the miracles already accomplished—until that great day when God will restore the true justice of His design in creation? If we pray about peace in the world, aren't we better equipped to be agents of reconciliation when we corporately recall that Christ has already broken down all the barriers between human beings with God and with each other by taking the separations into Himself on the cross and if we remember that someday all conflicts will cease in the culmination of His reign?

Language about the future in our culture is usually hopelessly pessimistic or else optimistic in a utopian way. It is essential that in our worship we recover the biblical language that provides an alternative vision. Both the language and the gestures of worship as outward actions form our inward character, so if our language about heaven realistically gives us hope, then we do not fall into the world's pessimism as we face the struggles of this broken, sinful present existence. On the other hand, our talk of heaven is not blind optimism, for heaven is not so much a place as a time and a Who—the eternal time of God's presence which has already broken into this present time through the atoning work of Christ.

The *Sanctus* as described above in section IX is one very eschatological hymn. When we teach worshipers the biblical source of this song, how it envisions God's reign in both the future and the present, and the cosmic choir with whom we are singing it, that will nurture their eschatological thinking and living. There are many contemporary settings of the *Sanctus* because churches and modern composers have realized how important its vision of God's eternal Lordship is.

Various seasons of the church year also are more conducive to making worship more eschatological. The entire Advent season, focusing on our preparation for Christ's coming, reminds us constantly of His coming again more deeply into our lives and His coming again in glory at the culmination of God's kingdom. Transfiguration Sunday (the last Sunday of the Epiphany season), when we recall the three disciples' experience in seeing Jesus in His fully divine glory, gives us a sustaining vision of the Kingdom before we enter Lent. Palm/Passion Sunday, when we remember the welcome Jesus received as he entered Jerusalem from those who lauded Him as king, can—in the tension of that

> **V**arious seasons of the church year also are more conducive to making worship more eschatological.

day with the Holy Week events that follow it—
remind us that Christ's kingship is not of this
world.

"All Saints Day," on November 1st, reminds us
that the saints who have gone before us are already exalting and exulting in their immersion in
God's presence. "Christ the King" Sunday, the
festival at the end of the church year, is perhaps
the most specific eschatological envisioning and
reminds us that every year leads toward the day
when all God's promises will be fulfilled and
Christ will rule over all. These are the times that
highlight eschatology, but actually every Sunday
is rich with potential for praising the LORD's coming and governing, for thereby recovering our eschatological hope, and for being formed to live
that hope in daily life.

One means for remembering is the Lord's Supper, for, as many denominations like to say, the
Communion is "a foretaste of the feast to come."
Jesus told His disciples that He would not eat of
this meal with them again until He ate it in the
fullness of God's kingdom (see Luke 22:14-20).
This awareness causes us to ask how well the sac-
ramental practices in our churches reflect our eschatology. How often in your worship services

do you savor this meal in anticipation of the heavenly feast? How well do you highlight the Lord's Supper as a major mark of your Christian identity?

Let us also consider the place of Baptism in our worship services and congregational life. Do we emphasize that Baptism is the beginning for the one baptized of the eternal reign of God in his or her life? Do we welcome those who are baptized into our congregational participation in the kingdom of God? Do we recognize as a community that it is the responsibility of all of us to be agents of God's nurturing and transforming work to create in those who are baptized an eschatological way of life?

How Eschatological Worship Will Form Us, Personally and Corporately, for the Sake of the World

It is especially important that our churches' sermons and songs and other elements of worship offer a better sense of the eschatological, for many people in our culture are looking for some sort of hope for the future—and because of the general distrust of institutions fostered in the '60s and still pervasive in our society, they do not

turn to churches to satisfy their spiritual yearn-
ings. That makes the daily and personal witness
of our conversation and lives more critically important, and we could be much better witnesses
to our neighbors if our worship formed us more
thoroughly to be conscious of the presence now
of God's future reign.

Our character as believers will be obviously
different if our worship forms us to live oriented
by the present and future reign of God. As an example, we will be formed to be dependent—in
contrast to our culture's insistence on always being in control. Both we as individuals and our
churches will be formed to be humble, instead of
competing to be successful. Eschatological worship will nurture us to be a people who are con-
trite for our mistakes and misdeeds, Joy-full in
the riches of God's forgiveness, and ardently en-
thusiastic about the LORD's guidance. We will be
aware of our insignificance (for God is the one
who reigns) and yet of our critical importance for
God's purposes. We will also be more conscious
of the unfathomed mastery of God's sovereignty
and yet of the mystery of His intimate compassion for us.

Think how it would change the witness of

members of our churches if our worship imbued us with the eschatological sense that each of us carries God's kingdom wherever we go. Does every single person in our churches know that we leave worship equipped and empowered to *be Church* throughout the week? (Remember that we don't "go to church"; instead we *are* the Church.) How could we more powerfully influence the society around us if each of us in our churches and all of us together had a profound sense that we bring with us God's presence in an eschatological envisioning of the future fulfillment of all the LORD's promises? Wouldn't we go to our jobs differently if we remembered that? Wouldn't we do our daily chores and speak with our neighbors differently? Wouldn't an eschatological sense change everything about our daily lives?

Living in the light of God's reign will give us the courage, the wisdom, and the power of the Spirit at work through us to love our neighbors more deeply. We will be more ready to care for

166

them in their sufferings. Worship that is eschatologically oriented will have equipped us not to escape, but to encounter the world's pain—for we will know that ultimately God's reign will do away with all sorrow and hardship, so we can be agents of His healing work now.

Similarly, an eschatological orientation frees us to confront sin and the powers of evil, for we know that Christ has already triumphed over them. Furthermore, worship continually reminds us that we are set free by God's forgiveness and changed by grace to re-

> **A**n eschatological orientation frees us to confront sin and the powers of evil, for we know that Christ has already triumphed over them.

pudiate sin, oppose evil, defeat oppressions, endure sufferings for the sake of others. Our present participation in God's future kingdom enables us to be realistic about the functioning of the principalities and powers in this world and time, for we confidently trust that Christ has already defeated them and that at the culmination of His kingdom God will annihilate them forever.

We live in a culture starved for genuine hope. Many people find their lives disoriented and hopeless as they feel threatened by many nations' militarism, overwhelmed by consumerist propaganda, frenzied by technological overkill, bereft of wholehearted relationships. Life often seems futureless.

Worship dare not be glib or superficial, ought not to dispense false assurances or manipulate emotions. Instead, genuine worship always offers the true hope of the Gospel—neither entertainment nor escapism, neither diversion nor another sort of consumerism, but the terrible truth about sin and evil and the even greater truth (in all its glory) that on the cross and through the empty tomb Christ has been victorious over iniquity, injury, and death. Worship will then enfold all of us who search for hope in God's present cosmic reign and challenge us to engage in God's sovereign purposes of ministry to the world. Finally, worship's celebration of God's governance will equip us with patience and endurance to endure the hardships of this life as we await the culmination of God's kingdom. This is all, indeed, good news for us each and together to tell our neighbors. Our goal is to bring the world to worship our God with us.

Finally, what kind of people should we be as

we wait for the LORD's coming? Since He is coming to judge the world in righteousness and faithfulness, may our worship form us to be such a community of justice and truth. If we truly worship the LORD of the heavens and the earth, we will be formed to be a community in His likeness—to speak the truth in a culture of lies, to work for justice in a world of disparity and oppressions, to care for the poor when the gap between rich and poor continues to widen, to resist the deceptions of our society and live in open integrity and honesty. In simple terms, may our worship form us to live as people of the kingdom of God. And that way of life, observed by our churches' neighbors, will give warrant for belief!

Let us pray: Triune God, may our worship always be directed to You. Teach us how to learn from Your Word and discover from Your Church throughout time and space how best to worship You. Guide each of us, Your people, and all of us together in our churches as we grapple with questions for the sake of being more faithful as Your Church in worship. May Your presence, encountered in worship, and the eschatological wisdom of the Scriptures form us, as individuals and as a community, to proclaim to the world around us the good news of Your reign. We pray this boldly because You have always been faithful to Your promises throughout the history of our forebears, and we are confident that the culmination of Your kingdom will bring the total fulfillment of all Your purposes. Use us as agents of Your governance to bring righteousness and faithfulness to our world. We ask this in the name of Jesus our Lord, whose coming we eagerly await so that we will at last worship You perfectly, and who reigns with You, Father, and the Holy Spirit, one God, now and forevermore. Amen.

Discussion Questions

INTRODUCTION

1. Does the worship of our church enable us to be like the clouds (see Heschel's poem) and ready to die for the sake of God's glory? How does it do that?
2. Does the worship of our church equip us to witness to our neighbors? In what ways?
3. Does the worship of our church deepen our desire to serve the world and minister to its needs? How does it equip us for that service?
4. What sorts of fights about worship do we have in our church? What causes them?
5. Before reading further in this book, what kinds of deeper questions do we think we should be asking about our church's worship?

SECTION I

1. What are the advantages of using words like *traditional* and *contemporary*? What are the disadvantages? What precisely do we mean by those words?
2. What might be some of the benefits in calling the Old Testament the "First Testament"? How does this phrase help us to see that God's character does not change between the two testaments?

3. What is the subject matter of the early Christian hymns that are in the Bible? What hymns or songs that we use today have the same subject matter?

4. What does the phrase _dialectical tension_ mean? How can we hold together two truths that are both very important and yet seem to be contradictory, without over-accentuating one side or the other?

5. Does our church over-accentuate one or the other side of the two necessities of Spirit and truth? How might we create a better balance of this dialectical pair?

6. Does the music in our church give us a sense of the whole Church throughout space and time? If not, what might we do to deepen that sense?

7. If faith is a language that we speak and live, how do we learn it? How does worship help to form our faith language?

SECTION II

1. Why is the name _LORD_ so important?

2. Is it possible truly to worship if we don't feel like it? How? Or why not?

3. How could our churches help us remember that worship is for God and not ourselves? How could we remember that more deeply in our personal lives?

4. What difference will it make in how and when we worship if we remember that worship is for God?

5. What factors cause churches to forget that worship is for God?

SECTION III

1. What does it mean to "bless God's name"? What implications does that phrase have for our daily lives?
2. Does our church follow the church year? Why or why not?
3. What are some benefits of following the church year? What are some disadvantages?
4. What are some examples of visual art that churches could use to highlight seasons of the church year?
5. How might music be different according to the season of the church year and the aspects of God's character upon which we are focusing?

SECTION IV

1. What is the difference between worship and evangelism? Why is that important? What, then, is the relationship of worship and evangelism?
2. How have churches confused worship and evangelism? What are some of the results?
3. What are some of the destructive elements of our cultural environment? What elements of our milieu support Christianity?
4. What are the seven marks of the Church in Acts 2:42-47? Is our church characterized by them all?

How could we develop our corporate life to be more like that of the early Christians?

5. Besides the phrase "going to church," what are some examples of bad theology that we speak and then live? How could we be more careful of our language and behavior?

SECTION V

1. Is Mammon a problem in our church? Why? What are some of the results?

2. What other idolatries characterize our congregation? With what idolatries do I struggle?

3. Why is the "fear of the LORD" important? Which side of the dialectic of fear and love does our church accentuate or do we have a good balance of the two?

4. What other dialectical pairs besides the ones listed should be kept balanced in the Christian faith and life? What would help us to keep them more balanced?

5. Why is it important to be strongly Trinitarian in the struggle against idolatries?

SECTION VI

1. Give an example of a song in which the text and the sound are not congruent. How might we change the song so that its meaning and its form match more closely?

2. Does our church effectively call forth the creative

gifts of members? In what ways could we increase the utilization of people's artistry?

3. How does our technological society's "quick-fix" mentality invade our church and its worship?

4. Do we use technology well in our church? How or how not?

5. What sorts of "commodities" do people want worship to provide? How could we enable them instead to "engage in the practice of worship"?

SECTION VII

1. What are some biblical names for God that we rarely use? How might thinking about them increase our appreciation for all that God is?

2. Why should worship be both contextual and classical? What are the dangers of over-accentuating one or the other of this dialectical pair?

3. What are some of the dangers if a church has too much liberty in the worship service? How might we keep a good balance of liturgical ordering and spontaneity?

4. In what ways does an accentuation primarily on intimacy with God or on the awe of God cause problems? How could we develop a better balance of both sides of this dialectic?

5. Why does the human psyche need ritual? How can we keep the church's rituals from becoming empty ritualism?

6. What kinds of percussion does our church use? Does it match the words we are singing? Is it helpful or harmful to the congregation's participation? How might our percussion become more supportive of genuine worship?

7. What instruments do we use in worship? Why? What other possibilities might we explore?

SECTION VIII

1. What were the high points of worship in the early Church? Why? What are they in our church? Do we need to change that? Why or why not? How might we make changes?

2. Which elements of the ancient Church's liturgy does our church utilize in worship? Why are those important to us?

3. Which elements of the ancient Church's liturgy does our church omit? Why are those not important to us?

4. What is the "liturgy" of our church? Which of the three trajectories listed at the end of the chapter have we primarily followed? Is there anything we would like to change? Why?

5. How might a knowledge of Church history help us deal with conflicts over worship?

SECTION IX

1. How might it change the way we worship if we think of every aspect of the service as our offering?

How might it change our daily lives to remember that everything is offering?

2. What difference has it made in the strength and character of churches that Christianity is no longer the dominant culture in North America?

3. How does our church give us a sense of the "great cloud of witnesses" in our worship services? How might a sense of the Church throughout space and time affect our daily lives?

4. Should we "dress up" for worship? Why or why not?

5. Why should we "tremble" before God? How will that affect our worship? our daily lives?

SECTION X

1. What does it mean that God is sovereign if we experience tragedies such as that of September 11, 2001? What does "the LORD reigns" mean in times of crisis?

2. How does worship "redescribe the world"? How does that affect our daily lives?

3. How does our church use the Scriptures in worship? How does our use of Scripture form our character as individuals and as a community? Is there anything we might change?

4. What Christian symbols does our worship space include? How do they help me worship? How do they form our lives? Do we need more symbols? less? Why?

5. What are the main questions we should keep asking about our church's worship? Why are these important?

SECTION XI

1. Give some favorite examples of the creation's praising. How do these examples increase our own praise?
2. Why does the LORD's coming call forth creation's praise?
3. Does our church engage in strong community life? Why or why not? How might we strengthen the communal life of our church?
4. Why is God's tri-unity important for our church's communal life?
5. What is a "charismacracy"? Does our congregation operate as a charismacracy? How might a deepened sense of the Trinity enable us to become more of a charismacracy?

SECTION XII

1. In what ways does the LORD come?
2. How does the sense that eternal life is our present possession affect our daily lives?
3. What are some practical ways we can be involved in extending God's kingdom?
4. How does an eschatological orientation help us "endure" suffering? What is the biblical meaning of endurance?

5. What does the word "awe-full" cause me to think about?

6. Is our church's worship very eschatologically oriented? Do we concentrate more on the "already" or the "not yet"? What would help us keep a good balance of the "already but not yet"? How might that affect our daily lives?

7. How does being eschatological help us to love our neighbors more deeply?

Notes

1. Abraham Joshua Heschel, *Man's Quest for God* (1954; reprint, Santa Fe, N.Mex.: Aurora Press, 1998), 5.
2. Throughout this book I will use capitalized *Church* to signify the ideal as Christ would have His Body be and uncapitalized *church* or *churches* to name concrete congregations, fallen and seeking-to-be-faithful realities, more or less living out what Church means.
3. See Robert E. Webber, *Ancient-Future Faith: Rethinking Evangelicalism for a Postmodern World* (Grand Rapids, Mich.: Baker, 1999).
4. See especially chapter 15, "Worship Is Not a Matter of Taste," and chapter 26, "Criteria by Which to Plan," in Marva J. Dawn, *A Royal "Waste" of Time: The Splendor of Worshiping God and Being Church for the World* (Grand Rapids, Mich.: Eerdmans, 1999).
5. See Christopher Lasch, *The Culture of Narcissism: American Life in an Age of Diminishing Expectations* (New York: Norton, 1978).
6. See, for example, Robert E. Webber, ed., *The Services of the Christian Year*, vol 5, *The Complete Li-*

brary of Christian Worship (Nashville, Tenn.: Star Song Publishing, 1994).

7. It is my custom to capitalize characteristic words to call attention to their special quality in the Christian life, as gifts from God and our relationship with Him. In this book the word *Joy* is capitalized to distinguish the specific Joy of the LORD from mere (and fading) human happiness. This is especially important for our discussion about worship issues because many churches strive to give participants an emotional "high" in worship, while I am concerned to equip them instead with a lasting Joy that will endure long after the worship excitement has faded and even when sorrows and hard times erase human happiness.

8. Douglas John Hall used this phrase in his plenary address for a Gospel and Our Culture Network conference in 1996. His presentation, "Metamorphosis: From Christendom to Diaspora," is available in *Confident Witness—Changing World: Rediscovering the Gospel in North America*, ed. Craig Van Gelder (Grand Rapids, Mich.: Eerdmans, 1999), 67–89.

9. See George R. Hunsberger, "Sizing Up the Shape of the Church," *The Church Between Gospel and Culture: The Emerging Mission in North America*, eds. George R. Hunsberger and Craig Van Gelder (Grand Rapids, Mich.: Eerdmans, 1996), 333–346.

10. This language is from Albert Borgmann's *Technol-*

ogy and the Character of Contemporary Life: A Philosophical Inquiry (Chicago: University of Chicago Press, 1984), especially pages 196–209. For an explanation of the "device paradigm," see Marva J. Dawn, *Unfettered Hope: A Call to Faithful Living in an Affluent Socity* (Louisville: Westminster John Knox Press, 2003).

11. Tony Jones, "Liberated by Reality," *Books and Culture* (September/October 1999): 27.

12. See Kenda Creasy Dean and Ron Foster, *The Godbearing Life: The Art of Soul Tending for Youth Ministry* (Nashville: Upper Room Books, 1998).

13. This example is from C. Peter Wagner, *Churchquake!: How the New Apostolic Reformation Is Shaking Up the Church as We Know It* (Ventura, Calif.: Regal Books, 1999), 155–182.

14. C. S. Lewis, *Letters to Malcolm: Chiefly on Prayer* (New York: Harcourt, Brace & World, 1964), 4.

15. Russell F. Mitman shows how this fourfold structure originates in Scripture and is followed in major denominations in *Worship in the Shape of Scripture* (Cleveland, Ohio: Pilgrim Press, 2001).

16. *Lutheran Book of Worship* (Minneapolis: Augsburg Publishing, 1978), 56.

17. See especially C. Welton Gaddy, *The Gift of Worship* (Nashville, Tenn.: Broadman and Holman, 1992).

18. This version is taken from *The Book of Common*

Prayer, used in the Episcopal Church and published by the Seabury Press, 1979, p. 362.

19. A superb guide to raising children to love worship is Robbie Castleman's *Parenting in the Pew: Guiding Your Children into the Joy of Worship*, rev. ed. (Downers Grove, Ill.: InterVarsity Press, 2002).

20. For a discussion of the gifts of Sabbath keeping, see Marva J. Dawn, *Keeping the Sabbath Wholly: Ceasing, Resting, Embracing, Feasting* (Grand Rapids, Mich.: Eerdmans, 1989).

21. My concern for this balance, for the sake of raising genuinely *Christian* children, was the reason for

writing *Is It a Lost Cause? Having the Heart of God for the Church's Children* (Grand Rapids, Mich.: Eerdmans, 1997).

22. For biblical exegesis and discussion questions for fostering deeper community, see Marva J. Dawn, *Truly the Community: Romans 12 and How to Be the Church* (Grand Rapids, Mich.: Eerdmans, 1992; re-issued 1997).

23. There is not space here to consider other false eschatologies, but they are contemplated more thoroughly in chapter 31, "Asking New and Old Questions as We Remember the Future," in Marva J. Dawn, *A Royal "Waste" of Time: The Splendor of Worshiping God and Being Church for the World* (Grand Rapids, Mich.: Eerdmans, 1999).

24. For an elaboration of how eschatology helps us deal with suffering, see Marva J. Dawn, *Joy in our Weakness: A Gift of Hope from the Book of Revelation*, rev. ed. (Grand Rapids, Mich.: Eerdmans, 2002).

Resources for Further Study and Group Discussion

Dawn, Marva J. *Reaching Out without Dumbing Down: A Theology of Worship for This Urgent Time*. Grand Rapids, Mich.: Eerdmans, 1995.

_____. *A Royal "Waste" of Time: The Splendor of Worshiping God and Being Church for the World*. Grand Rapids, Mich.: Eerdmans, 1999.

_____. *Truly the Community: Romans 12 and How to Be the Church*. Grand Rapids, Mich.: Eerdmans, 1997 (reissued).

Horton, Michael. *A Better Way: Rediscovering the Drama of God-Centered Worship*. Grand Rapids, Mich.: Baker, 2002.

Hustad, Donald P. *True Worship: Reclaiming the Wonder & Majesty*. Wheaton, Ill.: Harold Shaw, 1998.

Kelderman, Duane, et al. *Authentic Worship in a Changing Culture*. Grand Rapids, Mich.: CRC Publications, 1997.

Kenneson, Philip D. and James L. Street. *Selling Out the Church: The Dangers of Church Marketing.* Nashville: Abingdon, 1997.

Lathrop, Gordon W. *Holy Things: A Liturgical Theology.* Minneapolis: Augsburg, 1993.

Long, Thomas G. *Beyond the Worship Wars: Building Vital and Faithful Worship.* Bethesda, Md.: Alban Institute, 2001.

Mitman, Russell E. *Worship in the Shape of Scripture.* Cleveland: Pilgrim, 2001.

Saliers, Don E. *Worship Come to its Senses.* Nashville: Abingdon, 1996.

Stewart, Sonja M. and Jerome W. Berryman. *Young Children and Worship.* Louisville: John Knox, 1989.

Torrance, James B. *Worship, Community, and the Triune God of Grace.* Downers Grove, Ill.: InterVarsity, 1996.

Webber, Robert, ed. *The Complete Library of Christian Worship.* Nashville, Tenn.: Star Song, 1994. The seven volumes are *The Biblical Foundations of Christian Worship, Twenty Centuries of Christian Worship, The Renewal of Sunday Worship,* (vol. 4 in two books) *Music and the Arts in Christian Worship, The Services of the Christian Year, The Sacred Actions of Christian Worship,* and *The Ministries of Christian Worship.*

Wilson-Dickson, Andrew. *The Story of Christian Music: From Gregorian Chant to Black Gospel.* Minneapolis: Augsburg, 1996.

Topical Index

About the Author

Marva J. Dawn serves the global Church as a theologian, author, musician, and educator under Christians Equipped for Ministry and as Teaching Fellow in Spiritual Theology at Regent College in Vancouver, British Columbia. A scholar with four master's degrees and a Ph.D. in Christian Ethics and the Scriptures from the University of Notre Dame, Dr. Dawn has taught for clergy and worship conferences and at seminaries throughout the United States and Canada and in Australia, England, Hong Kong, Japan, Madagascar, Mexico, New Zealand, Poland, Singapore, and Scotland. She is also well-known and highly appreciated as a preacher and speaker for all ages and sometimes contributes to worship by means of her musical gifts.

Dr. Dawn is the author of more than fifteen books, including two on worship—*Reaching Out without Dumbing Down* and *A Royal "Waste" of Time*—which were honored by the Academy of Parish Clergy in their top ten recommended books in 1996 and 2000, respectively. Her 2001 book entitled *Powers, Weakness, and the Tabernacling of God* was honored with the 2002 *Christianity Today* Book Award in the category of The Church/Pastoral Leadership.

Marva is very happily married to Myron Sandberg; they reside in Washington State.

Vital Questions
CLEAR THINKING FOR FAITHFUL LIVING

□ □ □ □ □ □ □ □ □ □ □ □ □ □ □ □ □ □ □ □

The Vital Questions series investigates key issues that make a practical difference in how Christians think and act. Each book's goal is to provide substantial, accessible discussion of issues about which Christians need to know more.

Look for the Vital Questions series wherever fine Christian books are sold.

Is God Intolerant?
by Dan Taylor

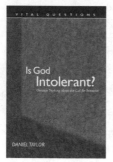

In contemporary culture, Christians have been called intolerant for standing up for what is right, for witnessing to other people about Jesus, and for stating that Jesus is the only way to God. In this volume, Dan Taylor, professor at Bethel College, explores the concept of tolerance. With depth and precision, he explains what true tolerance is and whether God wants Christians to be tolerant.

How *Shall* We Worship?
by Marva J. Dawn

If your church is like most churches, you have debated the value of various types of worship styles in your service—traditional versus contemporary, hymns versus praise songs. It's too easy for people to take sides in the worship wars. Marva Dawn will help you understand why there are so many disagreements in the church about worship. You'll never view worship the same after reading this book.

Does God Need Our Help?
by John F. Kilner and C. Ben Mitchell

Cloning. Assisted Suicide. Stem Cell Research. The advance of biotechnology today is breathtaking. But do we know where all of this is leading us? John F. Kilner and C. Ben Mitchell will lead you on a fascinating journey, explaining the cutting-edge advances in biotechnology. This book will help you formulate an informed and thoroughly Christian perspective on everything from assisted suicide to infertility treatments, from cloning to stem-cell research.